ITALIAN

in 10 minutes a day®

by Kristine K. Kershul, M.A., University of California, Santa Barbara

Consultants: Susan Worthington   Sabrina Tatta   Karen Manarolla Nordquist

Bilingual Books, Inc.

1719 West Nickerson Street, Seattle, WA 98119
Tel: (206) 284-4211 Fax: (206) 284-3660
www.10minutesaday.com • www.bbks.com

ISBN-13: 978-1-931873-06-2   First printing, April 2008

Can you say this?

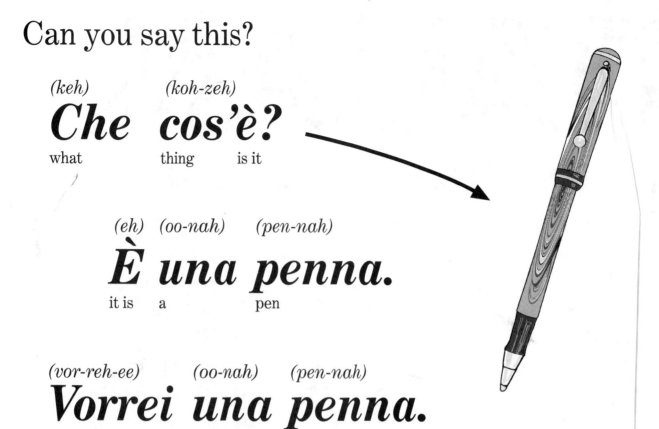

(keh)   *(koh-zeh)*
Che cos'è?
what   thing   is it

(eh)   *(oo-nah)*   *(pen-nah)*
È una penna.
it is   a   pen

(vor-reh-ee)   *(oo-nah)*   *(pen-nah)*
Vorrei una penna.
I would like

If you can say this, you can learn to speak Italian. You will be able to easily order win lunch, theater tickets, pastry, or anything else you wish. You simply ask **"Che cos'è?"** *(keh) (koh-zeh)* and, upon learning what it is, you can order it with **"Vorrei quello"** *(vor-reh-ee) (kwel-loh)*. Sounds easy, doesn't it?

The purpose of this book is to give you an **immediate** speaking ability in Italian. Using the acclaimed *"10 minutes a day®"* methodology, you will acquire a large work vocabulary that will suit your needs, and you will acquire it almost automatically. To a you, this book offers a unique and easy system of pronunciation above each word whic walks you through learning Italian.

If you are planning a trip or moving to where Italian is spoken, you will be leaps ahead of everyone if you take just a few minutes a day to learn the easy key words that this book offers. Start with Step 1 and don't skip around. Each day, work as far as you can comfortably go in those 10 minutes. Don't overdo it. Some days you might want to jus review. If you forget a word, you can always look it up in the glossary. Spend your firs 10 minutes studying the map on the previous page. And yes, have fun learning your new language.

As you work through the Steps, always use the special features which only this series offers. This book contains sticky labels and flash cards, free words, puzzles and quizze When you have completed this book, cut out the menu guide and take it along on your trip.

Throughout this book you will find an easy pronunciation guide above all new words. Refer to this Step whenever you need help, but remember, spend no longer than 10 minutes a day.

Most letters in Italian are identical to those in English. Many Italian letters are pronounced just as they are in English; however, others are pronounced quite differently.

To learn the sounds of the Italian letters, here is the entire alphabet. Practice these sounds with the examples given which are mostly towns or areas in Italy which you might visit. You can always refer back to these pages if you need to review.

Italian letter	English sound	Examples	Write it here
a	ah	**Catania** *(kah-tahn-yah)*	_____
b	b	**Brindisi** *(breen-dee-zee)*	_____
c *(before a, o, u, and all consonants)*	k	**Como** *(koh-moh)*	_____
c *(before e, i)*	ch	**Cefalù** *(cheh-fah-loo)*	_____
ch	k	**Chianti** *(kee-ahn-tee)*	_____
ci *(before a, o, u)*	ch	**Francia** *(frahn-chah)* France	_____
d	d	**Dolomiti** *(doh-loh-mee-tee)*	_____
e	*(as in let)* eh	**Elba** *(el-bah)*	_____
f	f	**Firenze** *(fee-ren-tseh)*	_____
g *(before a, o, u)*	*(as in go)* g	**Garda** *(gar-dah)*	_____
g *(before e, i)*	*(as in John)* j	**Genova** *(jeh-noh-vah)*	_____
gh	*(as in spaghetti)* g	**Ghirla** *(geer-lah)*	_____
gi *(before a, o, u)*	*(as in John)* j	**Giarre** *(jar-reh)*	_____
gl	*(as in million)* l-y	**Puglia** *(pool-yah)*	_____
h	always silent	**Heraclea** *(eh-rah-kleh-ah)*	_____
i *(varies)*	ee	**Amalfi** *(ah-mahl-fee)*	_____
	yah	**Italia** *(ee-tahl-yah)*	_____
j	y	**Jesi** *(yeh-zee)*	_____
k	k	**Khamma** *(kahm-mah)*	_____

Letter	Sound	Example	Write it here
l	l	**L**ombardia *(lohm-bar-dee-ah)*	_____
m	m	**M**ilano *(mee-lah-noh)*	_____
n	n	**N**apoli *(nah-poh-lee)*	_____
o	oh	**O**rvieto *(or-vee-eh-toh)*	_____
p	p	**P**adova *(pah-doh-vah)*	_____
qu*	kw	**Qu**arazza *(kwah-rah-tsah)*	_____
r	*(slightly rolled)* r	**R**oma *(roh-mah)*	_____
s *(varies)*	z	Pi**s**a *(pee-zah)*	Pisa, Pisa
	s	**S**iena *(see-eh-nah)*	_____
sc *(before a, o, u)*	sk	To**sc**ana *(toh-skah-nah)*	_____
sc *(before e, i)*	sh	**Sc**illa *(sheel-lah)*	_____
sch *(before e, i)*	sk	I**sch**ia *(eesk-yah)*	_____
sci *(before a, o, u)*	sh	Bre**sci**a *(breh-shah)*	_____
t	t	**T**orino *(toh-ree-noh)*	_____
u	oo	**U**mbria *(oom-bree-ah)*	_____
v	v	**V**enezia *(veh-neh-tsee-ah)*	_____
w	v	**W**elsberg *(velz-bairg)*	_____
x	ks	Colle di **X**omo *(kohl-leh)(dee)(ksoh-moh)*	_____
y	y	Courma**y**eur *(koor-my-yewr)*	_____
z *(varies)*	ts	La**z**io *(lah-tsee-oh)*	_____
	z	Vicen**z**a *(vee-chen-zah)*	_____
	dz	**Z**inola *(dzee-noh-lah)*	_____

*Just as in English, "**q**" is always joined with the letter "**u**." The letter "**u**" is then silent.

Double consonants such as **tt**, **pp**, **mm** and **ll** are emphasized in Italian. Don't hesitate to over-exaggerate them.

Sometimes the phonetics may seem to contradict your pronunciation guide. Don't panic! The easiest and best possible phonetics have been chosen for each individual word. Pronounce the phonetics just as you see them. Don't over-analyze them. Speak with an Italian accent and, above all, enjoy yourself!

When you arrive in **Italia** *(ee-tahl-yah)* the very first thing you will need to do is ask questions — "Where (**dove**) *(doh-veh)* is the bus stop?" "**Dove** *(doh-veh)* can I exchange money?" "**Dove** *(doh-veh)* is the lavatory?" "**Dove** *(doh-veh)* is a restaurant?" "**Dove** *(doh-veh)* do I catch a taxi?" "**Dove** is a good hotel?" " **Dove** is my luggage?" — and the list will go on and on for the entire length of your visit. In Italian, there are SEVEN KEY QUESTION WORDS to learn. For example, the seven key question words will help you find out exactly what you are ordering in a restaurant before you order it — and not after the surprise (or shock!) arrives. Notice that only one letter is different in the Italian words for "what" and "who." Don't confuse them! Take a few minutes to study and practice saying the seven key question words listed below. Then cover the Italian with your hand and fill in each of the blanks with the matching **parola** *(pah-roh-lah)* **italiana.** *(ee-tahl-yah-nah)*

(doh-veh) **DOVE** = WHERE _dove, dove, dove, dove_

(keh) **CHE** = WHAT _____

(kee) **CHI** = WHO _____

(pair-keh) **PERCHÉ** = WHY _____

(kwahn-doh) **QUANDO** = WHEN _____

(koh-meh) **COME** = HOW _____

(kwahn-toh) **QUANTO** = HOW MUCH _____

5

Now test yourself to see if you really can keep these **parole** *(pah-roh-leh)* straight in your mind. Draw lines
words
between the Italian **e** *(eh)* English equivalents below.
and

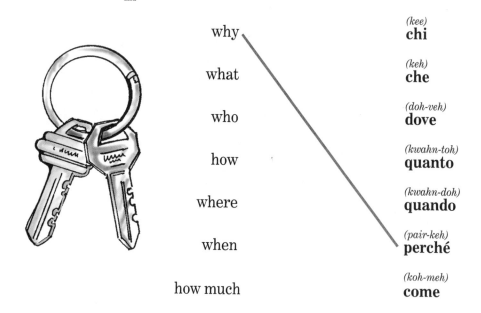

why — **chi** *(kee)*

what — **che** *(keh)*

who — **dove** *(doh-veh)*

how — **quanto** *(kwahn-toh)*

where — **quando** *(kwahn-doh)*

when — **perché** *(pair-keh)*

how much — **come** *(koh-meh)*

Examine the following questions containing these **parole** *(pah-roh-leh)*. Practice the sentences out loud **e** *(eh)*
and
then practice by copying the Italian in the blanks underneath each question.

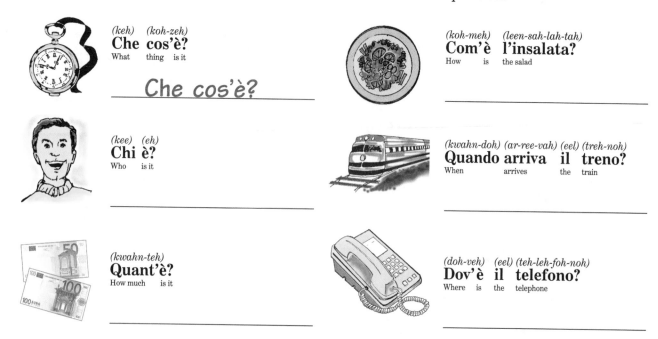

Che cos'è? *(keh) (koh-zeh)*
What   thing is it

Che cos'è?

Chi è? *(kee) (eh)*
Who   is it

_____

Quant'è? *(kwahn-teh)*
How much   is it

_____

Com'è l'insalata? *(koh-meh) (leen-sah-lah-tah)*
How   is   the salad

_____

Quando arriva il treno? *(kwahn-doh) (ar-ree-vah) (eel) (treh-noh)*
When   arrives   the   train

_____

Dov'è il telefono? *(doh-veh) (eel) (teh-leh-foh-noh)*
Where is   the   telephone

_____

"Dove" *(doh-veh)* will be your most used question **parola**. Say each of the following Italian sentences
aloud. Then write out each sentence without looking at the example. If you don't succeed on
the first try, don't give up. Just practice each sentence until you are able to do it easily.
Remember, **"ce"** is pronounced "cheh" and **"ci"** is pronounced "chee."

(soh-noh) (ee) (gah-bee-net-tee)
Dove sono i gabinetti?
Where are the restrooms

(doh-veh) (eel) (bahn-yoh)
Dov'è il bagno?
Where is the bathroom

SIGNORE SIGNORI

(doh-veh) (eel) (tahs-see)
Dov'è il tassì?
Where is the taxi

(doh-veh) (lah-oo-toh-boos)
Dov'è l' autobus?
Where is the bus

Dov'è il tassì?

_____ _____ _____

(eel) (ree-stoh-rahn-teh)
Dov'è il ristorante?
the restaurant

(lah) (bahn-kah)
Dov'è la banca?
the bank

(lahl-bair-goh)
Dov'è l' albergo?
hotel

_____ _____ _____

(see)
Sì, you can see similarities between *(een-gleh-zeh)* **inglese** and *(ee-tahl-yah-noh)* **italiano** if you look closely. You will be
yes   English   Italian

amazed at the number of *(pah-roh-leh)* **parole** which are identical (or almost identical) in both languages.
                        words

Of course, they do not always sound the same when spoken by an Italian speaker, but the

(see-mee-lee-too-dee-nee)
similitudini will certainly surprise you *(eh)* **e** make your work here easier. Listed below are five
similarities

"free" **parole** beginning with " *(ah)* **a** " to help you get started. Be sure to say each **parola** aloud *(eh)* **e**

then write out the **parole italiane** *(ee-tahl-yah-neh)* in the blanks to the right.
            words   Italian

☑ **l'alcool** *(lahl-kohl)*	alcohol	l'alcool, l'alcool, l'alcool, l'alcool
☐ **le Alpi** *(leh)(ahl-pee)*	Alps	_____
☐ **americano** *(ah-meh-ree-kah-noh)*	American	**a** _____
☐ **l'animale** *(lah-nee-mah-leh)*	animal	_____
☐ **l'appartamento** *(lahp-par-tah-men-toh)*	apartment	_____

Free **parole** like these will appear at the bottom of the following pages in a yellow color band.

They are easy — enjoy them! Remember, in Italian, **"ch"** is pronounced "k."

7

(een) (ee-tahl-yah-noh)
In italiano there are multiple **parole** for "the" and "a," but they are very easy. If the Italian
in Italian words

word ends in "**a**" (feminine) it *usually* will have the article "**la.**" If the word ends in "**o**" (masculine)

it *usually* will have the article "**il**" or "**lo.**" Study these patterns below.

(eel) (rah-gah-tsoh)
il ragazzo
the boy

(ee) (rah-gah-tsee)
i ragazzi
the boys

(lah) (rah-gah-tsah)
la ragazza
the girl

(leh) (rah-gah-tseh)
le ragazze
the girls

(loh) (spek-kee-oh)
lo specchio
the mirror

(l-yee) (spek-kee)
gli specchi
the mirrors

(oon) (seen-yoh-reh)
un signore
a man

(deh-ee) (seen-yoh-ree)
dei signori
some men

(oo-nah) (seen-yoh-rah)
una signora
a lady

(del-leh) (seen-yoh-reh)
delle signore
some ladies

(oo-noh) (strah-nee-eh-roh)
uno straniero
a foreigner

(del-yee) (strah-nee-eh-ree)
degli stranieri
some foreigners

(een-gleh-zeh)
This might appear difficult, but only because it is different from **inglese.** Just remember you will

be understood whether you say "**il ragazzo**" or "**la ragazzo.**" Soon you will automatically select

the right one without even thinking about it.

In Step 2 you were introduced to the Seven Key
QuestionWords. These seven words are the basics, the
most essential building blocks for learning Italian.
Throughout this book you will come across keys
asking you to fill in the missing question word. Use
this opportunity not only to fill in the blank on that
key, but to review all your question words. Play with
the new sounds, speak slowly and have fun.

☐ **l'appetito** *(lahp-peh-tee-toh)*	appetite	_____
☐ **aprile** *(ah-pree-leh)*	April	_____
☐ **l'arrivo** *(lar-ree-voh)*	arrival	**a** _____
☐ **l'attenzione** *(laht-ten-tsee-oh-neh)*	attention	_____
☐ **l'attore** *(laht-toh-reh)*	actor	_____

Before you proceed with this Step, situate yourself comfortably in your living room. Now look

around you. Can you name the things that you see in this **stanza** *(stahn-zah)* in Italian? You can probably

<small>room</small>

guess **la lampada** *(lahm-pah-dah)* and maybe even **il tavolo.** *(tah-voh-loh)* Let's learn the rest of them. After practicing

<small>lamp</small>   <small>table</small>

these **parole** out loud, write them in the blanks below.

(fee-neh-strah)
la finestra
<small>window</small>

(lahm-pah-dah)
la lampada ————————————
<small>lamp</small>

(soh-fah)
il sofà ————————————
<small>sofa</small>

(seh-dee-ah)
la sedia ————————————
<small>chair</small>

(tahp-peh-toh)
il tappeto ————————————
<small>carpet</small>

(tah-voh-loh)
il tavolo ———— *il tavolo, il tavolo* ————
<small>table</small>

(por-tah)
la porta ————————————
<small>door</small>

(loh-roh-loh-joh)
l' orologio ————————————
<small>clock</small>

(ten-dee-nah)
la tendina ————————————
<small>curtain</small>

(teh-leh-foh-noh)
il telefono ————————————
<small>telephone</small>

(kwah-droh)
il quadro
<small>picture</small>

You will notice that the correct form of **il**, *(eel)* **la**, **l'** or **lo** is given **con** *(kohn)* each noun. This is for your

                                                          <small>with</small>

(een-for-mah-tsee-oh-neh)
informazione — just remember to use one of them. Now open your book to the sticky labels
<small>information</small>

on page 17 and later on page 35. Peel off the first 11 labels **e** *(eh)* proceed around **la stanza,** *(stahn-zah)* labeling

                                                                                    <small>room</small>

these items in your home. This will help to increase your Italian **parola** power easily. Don't

forget to say each **parola** as you attach the label.

Now ask yourself, **"Dov'è la lampada?"** *(doh-veh)* **e** *(eh)* point at it while you answer, **"Ecco la lampada."** *(ek-koh)*

                                                                                          <small>here is</small>

Continue on down the **lista** *(lee-stah)* above until you feel comfortable with these new **parole.**

                                   <small>list</small>

❒	**la baia** *(bah-ee-ah)*	bay	————————
❒	**il balcone** *(bahl-koh-neh)*	balcony	————————
❒	**la banana** *(bah-nah-nah)*	banana **b**	————————
❒	**la banca** *(bahn-kah)*	bank	————————
❒	**la benedizione** *(beh-neh-dee-tsee-oh-neh)*	benediction	————————

(lah) (kah-zah)
la casa = the house

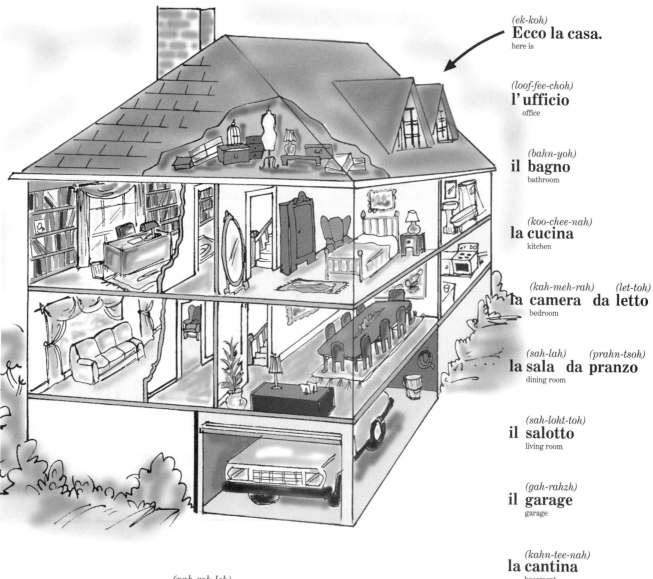

(ek-koh)
Ecco la casa.
here is

(loof-fee-choh)
l'ufficio
office

(bahn-yoh)
il bagno
bathroom

(koo-chee-nah)
la cucina
kitchen

(kah-meh-rah) *(let-toh)*
la camera da letto
bedroom

(sah-lah) *(prahn-tsoh)*
la sala da pranzo
dining room

(sah-loht-toh)
il salotto
living room

(gah-rahzh)
il garage
garage

(kahn-tee-nah)
la cantina
basement

(pah-roh-leh)
While learning these new **parole,** let's not forget:

(lah-oo-toh) (mahk-kee-nah)
l'auto / la macchina
automobile

(moh-toh-chee-klet-tah)
la motocicletta / la moto
motorcycle

(bee-chee-klet-tah) (bee-chee)
la bicicletta / la bici
bicycle

_____   _____   _____

❏ **il biscotto** *(bee-skoht-toh)*	biscuit, cookie	_____
❏ **la bistecca** *(bee-stek-kah)*	beefsteak	_____
❏ **la bottiglia** *(boht-teel-yah)*	bottle **b**	_____
❏ **breve** *(breh-veh)*	brief, short	_____
❏ **brillante** *(breel-lahn-teh)*	brilliant, shining	_____

(gaht-toh)
il gatto
cat

(jar-dee-noh)
il giardino
garden

(fee-oh-ree)
i fiori
flowers

il giardino, il giardino

(kah-neh)
il cane
dog

(boo-kah) (del-leh) (let-teh-reh)
la buca delle lettere
mailbox

(poh-stah)
la posta
mail

Peel off the next set of labels **e** *(eh)* wander through your **casa** *(kah-zah)* learning these new **parole.** *(pah-roh-leh)* It will be somewhat difficult to label **il gatto,** *(gaht-toh)* cat **i fiori** *(fee-oh-ree)* flowers **o** *(oh)* or **il cane,** *(kah-neh)* dog but be creative. Practice by asking yourself, **"Dov'è l'auto?"** *(lah-oo-toh)* car and reply, **"Ecco l'auto."** here is

Dov'è la casa?

☐	**la capitale** *(kah-pee-tah-leh)*	capital	
☐	**il castello** *(kah-stel-loh)*	castle	
☐	**la categoria** *(kah-teh-goh-ree-ah)*	category	**c**
☐	**la cattedrale** *(kaht-teh-drah-leh)*	cathedral	
☐	**il centro** *(chen-troh)*	center, downtown	

5 *(oo-noh)* *(doo-eh)* *(treh)*
Uno, Due, Tre
one two three

Consider for a minute how important numbers are. How could you tell someone your phone number, your address **o** *(oh)* or your hotel room if you had no numbers? And think of how difficult it would be if you could not understand the time, the price of a cappuccino **o** the correct bus to take. When practicing the **numeri** *(noo-meh-ree)* numbers below, notice the similarities which have been underlined for you between **quattro** *(kwaht-troh)* four and **quattordici,** *(kwaht-tor-dee-chee)* fourteen **sette** *(set-teh)* seven and **diciassette** *(dee-chahs-set-teh)* seventeen **e** so on.

0	**zero** *(zeh-roh)*	_____	10	**dieci** *(dee-eh-chee)*	_____
1	**<u>uno</u>** *(oo-noh)*	_____	11	**<u>undici</u>** *(oon-dee-chee)*	_____
2	**<u>due</u>** *(doo-eh)*	_____	12	**<u>dodici</u>** *(doh-dee-chee)*	_____
3	**<u>tre</u>** *(treh)*	_____	13	**<u>tredici</u>** *(treh-dee-chee)*	_____
4	**<u>quattro</u>** *(kwaht-troh)*	_____	14	**<u>quattordici</u>** *(kwaht-tor-dee-chee)*	_____
5	**<u>cinque</u>** *(cheen-kweh)*	_____	15	**<u>quindici</u>** *(kween-dee-chee)*	_____
6	**<u>sei</u>** *(seh-ee)*	_____	16	**<u>sedici</u>** *(seh-dee-chee)*	_____
7	**<u>sette</u>** *(set-teh)*	*sette, sette, sette*	17	**<u>diciassette</u>** *(dee-chahs-set-teh)*	_____
8	**<u>otto</u>** *(oht-toh)*	_____	18	**<u>diciotto</u>** *(dee-choht-toh)*	_____
9	**<u>nove</u>** *(noh-veh)*	_____	19	**<u>diciannove</u>** *(dee-chahn-noh-veh)*	_____
10	**dieci** *(dee-eh-chee)*	_____	20	**venti** *(ven-tee)*	_____

☑ **la cerimonia** *(cheh-ree-moh-nee-ah)* . . . . ceremony   **c**   *la cerimonia, la cerimonia*
☐ **certo** *(chair-toh)* . . . . certainly
☐ **il cinema** *(chee-neh-mah)* . . . . cinema, movie house
☐ **il cioccolato** *(chohk-koh-lah-toh)* . . . . chocolate
☐ **la comunicazione** *(koh-moo-nee-kah-tsee-oh-neh)* communication

(oo-zee) **Usi** these *(noo-meh-ree)* **numeri** on a daily basis. Count to yourself *(een)* **in italiano** when you brush your teeth,
use numbers in Italian

exercise *(oh)* **o** commute to work. Fill in the blanks below according to the **numeri** given in
numbers

parentheses. Now is also a good time to learn these two very important phrases.

(vor-reh-ee)
vorrei ———————————————————————————————
I would like

(vor-rem-moh)
vorremmo ———————————————————————————————
we would like

(vor-reh-ee) **Vorrei** _____ (1) I would like	*(bee-skoht-toh)* **biscotto.** biscuit	*(kwahn-tee)* **Quanti?** _____ (1) how many
Vorrei _____ (7)	*(frahn-koh-bohl-lee)* **francobolli.** stamps	**Quanti?** _____ (7)
(vor-reh-ee) **Vorrei** _____ (8)	**francobolli.** stamps	**Quanti?** _____ (8)
Vorrei _____ (5)	**francobolli.**	**Quanti?** __cinque__ (5)
(vor-rem-moh) **Vorremmo** _____ (9) we would like	*(kar-toh-lee-neh)* **cartoline.** postcards	*(kwahn-teh)* **Quante?** _____ (9)
Vorremmo _____ (10) we would like	*(kar-toh-lee-neh)* **cartoline.**	*(kwahn-teh)* **Quante?** _____ (10)
Vorrei _____ (1)	*(beel-yet-toh)* **biglietto.** ticket	**Quanti?** _____ (1)
(vor-rem-moh) **Vorremmo** _____ (4)	*(beel-yet-tee)* **biglietti.** tickets	**Quanti?** _____ (4)
Vorremmo _____ (11)	*(beel-yet-tee)* **biglietti.**	**Quanti?** _____ (11)
(vor-reh-ee) **Vorrei** _____ (3)	*(teh)* **tè.** tea	**Quanti?** _____ (3)
Vorremmo _____ (4)	*(beek-kee-eh-ree)(dah-kwah)* **bicchieri d'acqua.** glasses of water	(how many) _____ (4)

☐	**la conservazione** *(kohn-sair-vah-tsee-oh-neh)*	conservation
☐	**la conversazione** *(kohn-vair-sah-tsee-oh-neh)*	conversation
☐	**il coraggio** *(koh-rah-joh)*	courage **c**
☐	**la cugina** *(koo-jee-nah)*	female cousin
☐	**il cugino** *(koo-jee noh)*	male cousin

13

Now see if you can translate the following thoughts into **italiano.** The answers are provided

Italian

(pah-jee-nah)

upside down at the bottom of the **pagina.**

page

1. I would like seven postcards.

_____

2. I would like nine stamps.

_____

3. We would like four cups of tea.

_____

4. We would like three tickets.

_____

Review **i numeri** 1 through 20. Write out your telephone number, fax number *(eh)* **e** cellular

number. Then write out a friend's telephone number and a relative's telephone number.

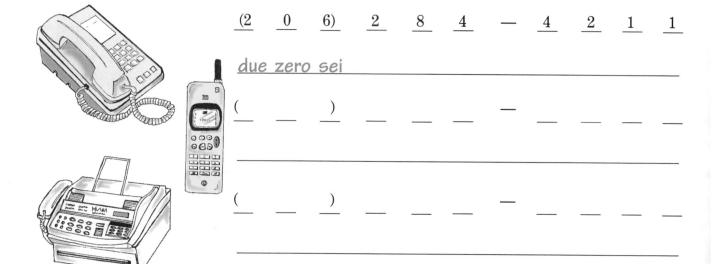

(2   0   6)   2   8   4   —   4   2   1   1

due zero sei _____

(___) ___ ___ ___ — ___ ___ ___ ___

_____

(___) ___ ___ ___ — ___ ___ ___ ___

_____

RISPOSTE CORRETTE

1. Vorrei sette cartoline.
2. Vorrei nove francobolli.
3. Vorremmo quattro tè.
4. Vorremmo tre biglietti.

(ee) *(koh-loh-ree)* *(soh-noh)* *(een)* *(ee-tahl-yah)* *(ah-meh-ree-kah)*
I colori sono the same **in Italia** as they are **in America** — they just have different
colors · are · in

(noh-mee) *(vee-oh-let-toh)*
nomi. You can easily recognize **violetto** as violet. Let's learn the basic **colori** so when you are
names

(kah-zah)
invited to someone's **casa e** you want to bring flowers, you will be able to order the color you
house

want. Once you've learned **i colori,** quiz yourself. What color are your shoes? Your eyes?

Your hair? Your house?

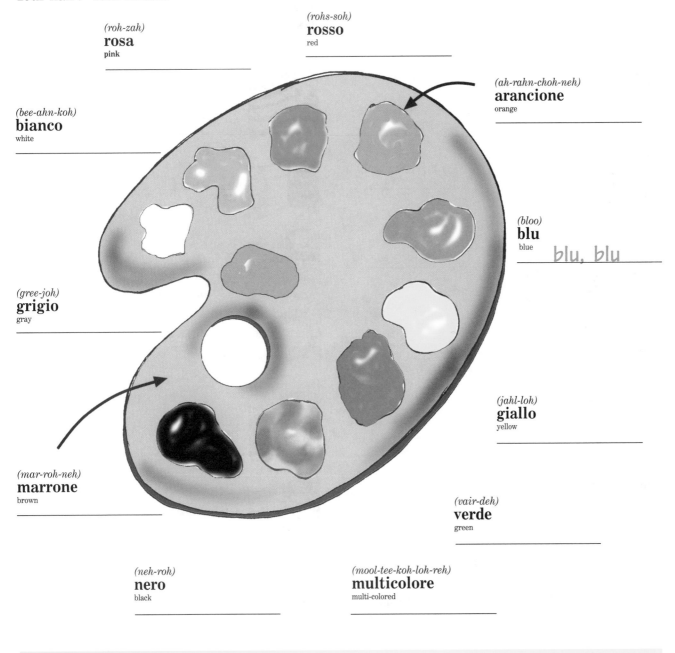

(roh-zah)
rosa
pink

(rohs-soh)
rosso
red

(ah-rahn-choh-neh)
arancione
orange

(bee-ahn-koh)
bianco
white

(bloo)
blu
blue
blu, blu

(gree-joh)
grigio
gray

(jahl-loh)
giallo
yellow

(mar-roh-neh)
marrone
brown

(vair-deh)
verde
green

(neh-roh)
nero
black

(mool-tee-koh-loh-reh)
multicolore
multi-colored

❏ **la danza** *(dahn-tsah)*	dance	
❏ **decorato** *(deh-koh-rah-toh)*	decorated	
❏ **delizioso** *(deh-lee-tsee-oh-zoh)*	delicious	**d**
❏ **denso** *(den-soh)*	dense	
❏ **il desiderio** *(deh-zee-deh-ree-oh)*	desire, wish	

Peel off the next group of labels **e** proceed to label these **colori** in your **casa**. Identify the two **o**
                                                                                              house

three dominant colors in the flags below.

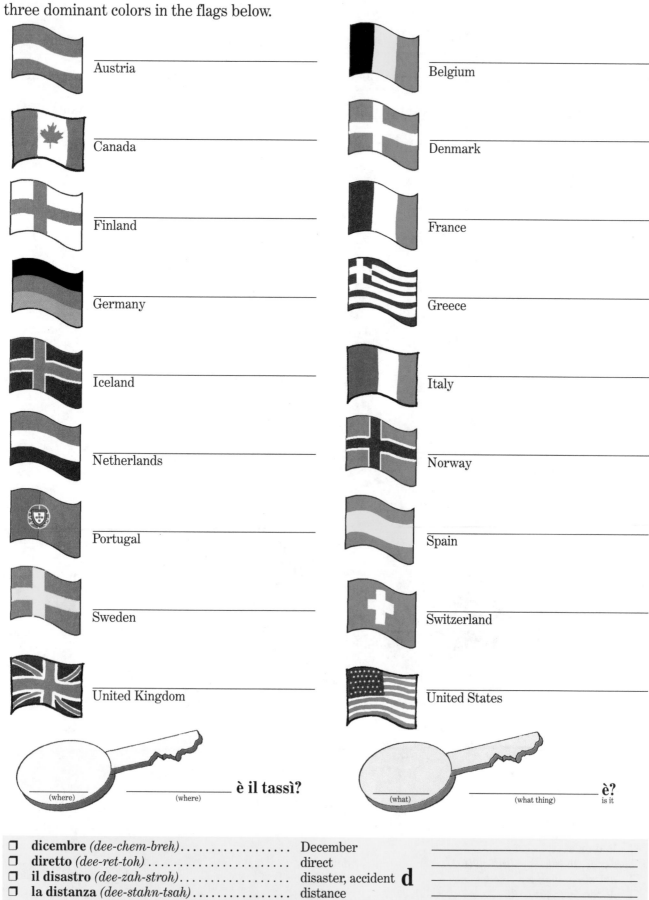

Austria _____

Belgium _____

Canada _____

Denmark _____

Finland _____

France _____

Germany _____

Greece _____

Iceland _____

Italy _____

Netherlands _____

Norway _____

Portugal _____

Spain _____

Sweden _____

Switzerland _____

United Kingdom _____

United States _____

_____ _____ **è il tassì?**
(where)   (where)

_____ _____ **è?**
(what)   (what thing)   is it

❏ **dicembre** *(dee-chem-breh)* . . . . December _____
❏ **diretto** *(dee-ret-toh)* . . . . direct _____
❏ **il disastro** *(dee-zah-stroh)* . . . . disaster, accident **d** _____
❏ **la distanza** *(dee-stahn-tsah)* . . . . distance _____
16 ❏ **divino** *(dee-vee-noh)* . . . . divine _____

(lahm-pah-dah) **la lampada**	*(mahk-kee-nah)* **la macchina**	*(mar-roh-neh)* **marrone**	*(laht-teh)* **il latte**
(soh-fah) **il sofà**	*(moh-toh)* **la moto**	*(rohs-soh)* **rosso**	*(boor-roh)* **il burro**
(seh-dee-ah) **la sedia**	*(bee-chee)* **la bici**	*(roh-zah)* **rosa**	*(sah-leh)* **il sale**
(tahp-peh-toh) **il tappeto**	*(gaht-toh)* **il gatto**	*(ah-rahn-choh-neh)* **arancione**	*(peh-peh)* **il pepe**
(tah-voh-loh) **il tavolo**	*(jar-dee-noh)* **il giardino**	*(bee-ahn-koh)* **bianco**	*(beek-kee-eh-reh)* *(vee-noh)* **il bicchiere di vino**
(por-tah) **la porta**	*(fee-oh-ree)* **i fiori**	*(jahl-loh)* **giallo**	*(beek-kee-eh-reh)* **il bicchiere**
(loh-roh-loh-joh) **l'orologio**	*(kah-neh)* **il cane**	*(gree-joh)* **grigio**	*(jor-nah-leh)* **il giornale**
(ten-dee-nah) **la tendina**	*(boo-kah)* *(del-leh)* *(let-teh-reh)* **la buca delle lettere**	*(neh-roh)* **nero**	*(tah-tsah)* **la tazza**
(teh-leh-foh-noh) **il telefono**	*(poh-stah)* **la posta**	*(bloo)* **blu**	*(kook-kee-eye-oh)* **il cucchiaio**
(fee-neh-strah) **la finestra**	*(zeh-roh)* 0 **zero**	*(vair-deh)* **verde**	*(kohl-tel-loh)* **il coltello**
(kwah-droh) **il quadro**	*(oo-noh)* 1 **uno**	*(mool-tee-koh-loh-reh)* **multicolore**	*(toh-vahl-yoh-loh)* **il tovagliolo**
(kah-zah) **la casa**	*(doo-eh)* 2 **due**	*(bwohn)* *(jor-noh)* **buon giorno**	*(for-ket-tah)* **la forchetta**
(loof-fee-choh) **l'ufficio**	*(treh)* 3 **tre**	*(bwoh-nah)* *(seh-rah)* **buona sera**	*(pee-aht-toh)* **il piatto**
(bahn-yoh) **il bagno**	*(kwaht-troh)* 4 **quattro**	*(bwoh-nah)* *(noht-teh)* **buona notte**	*(lar-mah-dee-et-toh)* **l'armadietto**
(koo-chee-nah) **la cucina**	*(cheen-kweh)* 5 **cinque**	*(chow)* **ciao**	*(teh)* **il tè**
(kah-meh-rah) *(let-toh)* **camera da letto**	*(seh-ee)* 6 **sei**	*(koh-meh)* *(stah)* **Come sta?**	*(kahf-feh)* **il caffè**
(sah-lah) *(prahn-tsoh)* **a sala da pranzo**	*(set-teh)* 7 **sette**	*(free-goh-ree-feh-roh)* **il frigorifero**	*(pah-neh)* **il pane**
(sah-loht-toh) **il salotto**	*(oht-toh)* 8 **otto**	*(koo-chee-nah)* **la cucina**	*(pair)* *(fah-voh-reh)* **per favore**
(gah-rahzh) **il garage**	*(noh-veh)* 9 **nove**	*(vee-noh)* **il vino**	*(grah-tsee-eh)* **grazie**
(kahn-tee-nah) **la cantina**	*(dee-eh-chee)* 10 **dieci**	*(beer-rah)* **la birra**	*(mee)* *(skoo-zee)* **mi scusi**

STICKY LABELS

This book has over 150 special sticky labels for you to use as you learn new words. When you are introduced to one of these words, remove the corresponding label from these pages. Be sure to use each of these unique self-adhesive labels by adhering them to a picture, window, lamp, or whatever object they refer to. And yes, they are removable! The sticky labels make learning to speak Italian much more fun and a lot easier than you ever expected. For example, when you look in the mirror and see the label, say

(spek-kee-oh)
"lo specchio."
mirror
⟶

Don't just say it once, say it again and again. And once you label the refrigerator, you should never again open that door without saying

(free-goh-ree-feh-roh)
"il frigorifero."
refrigerator

By using the sticky labels, you not only learn new words, but friends and family learn along with you! The sooner you start, the sooner you can use these labels at home or work.

7   *(eel) (deh-nah-roh)* **Il Denaro**
money

Before starting this Step, go back and review Step 5. It is important that you can count to

(ven-tee)
venti without looking at **il libro.** Let's learn the larger **numeri** now. After practicing aloud
twenty   *(lee-broh)*   *(noo-meh-ree)*
                     book

i numeri italiani below, write these **numeri** in the blanks provided. Again, notice the

(see-mee-lee-too-dee-nee)   *(kwaht-troh)*   *(kwaht-tor-dee-chee)*
similitudini   (underlined) between **numeri** such as **quattro** (4), **quattordici** (14),

(kwah-rahn-tah)   *(eh) (kwaht-troh-mee-lah)*
quaranta (40) **e quattromila** (4000).

10	*(dee-eh-chee)* **dieci** _____	1.000	*(meel-leh)* **mille** _____
20	*(ven-tee)* **venti** _____	2.000	*(doo-eh-mee-lah)* **duemila** _____
30	*(tren-tah)* **trenta** *trenta, trenta*	3.000	**tremila** _____
40	*(kwah-rahn-tah)* **quaranta** _____	4.000	**quattromila** _____
50	*(cheen-kwahn-tah)* **cinquanta** _____	5.000	**cinquemila** _____
60	*(ses-sahn-tah)* **sessanta** _____	6.000	**seimila** _____
70	*(set-tahn-tah)* **settanta** _____	7.000	**settemila** _____
80	*(oht-tahn-tah)* **ottanta** _____	8.000	**ottomila** _____
90	*(noh-vahn-tah)* **novanta** _____	9.000	**novemila** _____
100	*(chen-toh)* **cento** _____	10.000	*(dee-eh-chee-mee-lah)* **diecimila** _____
500	*(cheen-kweh-chen-toh)* **cinquecento** _____	10.500	**diecimilacinquecento** _____
1.000	*(meel-leh)* **mille** _____	11.000	*(oon-dee-chee-mee-lah)* **undicimila** _____

(ek-koh)
Ecco due important phrases to go with all these **numeri.** Say them out loud over and over and
here are

then write them out twice as many times.

(oh)
ho _____
I have

(ahb-bee-ah-moh)
abbiamo _____
we have

❐   **il dizionario** *(dee-tsee-oh-nah-ree-oh)* .... dictionary   _____
❐   **il dollaro** *(dohl-lah-roh)* .... dollar   _____
❐   **il dottore** *(doht-toh-reh)* .... doctor   **d**   _____
❐   **il dubbio** *(doob-bee-oh)* .... doubt   _____
❐   **durante** *(doo-rahn-teh)* .... during   _____

The unit of currency **in Italia** *(ee-tahl-yah)* **è l'euro,** *(leh-oo-roh)* abbreviated "**€**". Let's learn the various kinds of
(moh-neh-teh) (eh) (beel-yet-tee)
monete   e   biglietti. Always be sure to practice each **parola** out loud. You might want to

coins   bills

exchange some money **adesso** *(ah-des-soh)* so that you can familiarize yourself **con** *(kohn)* the various types of

now   with

denaro. *(deh-nah-roh)*

money

Biglietti *(beel-yet-tee)*   ## Monete *(moh-neh-teh)*

(cheen-kweh)(eh-oo-roh)
cinque   euro

(dee-eh-chee)
dieci   euro

(ven-tee)
venti euro

(cheen-kwahn-tah)
cinquanta euro

(chen-toh)
cento euro

100

(ven-tee) (chen-teh-see-mee)
venti centesimi

(cheen-kwahn-tah)
cinquanta   centesimi

(oon)(eh-oo-roh)
un euro

(doo-eh)
due euro

❏ **eccellente** *(eh-chel-len-teh)* .... excellent
❏ **l'economia** *(leh-koh-noh-mee-ah)* .... economy
❏ **l'entrata** *(len-trah-tah)* .... entrance   **e** _____
❏ **est** *(est)* .... east
❏ **Europa** *(eh-oo-roh-pah)* .... Europe

_____
_____
_____
_____

Review **i numeri dieci** *(dee-eh-chee)* through **mille** *(meel-leh)* again. **Adesso,** *(ah-des-soh)* how do you say "twenty-two" **o** "fifty-three" **in** *(een)* **italiano?** Put the numbers together in a logical sequence just as you do in English. See if you can say **e** write out **i numeri** on this **pagina.** *(pah-jee-nah)* page **Le risposte** *(ree-spoh-steh)* **sono** *(soh-noh)* are at the bottom of **la pagina.**

1. _____
   (25 = 20 + 5)

2. _____
   (83 = 80 + 3)

3. _____
   (47 = 40 + 7)

4. _____
   (96 = 90 + 6)

Adesso, *(ah-des-soh)* how would you say the following **in italiano?**

5. _____
   (I have 8.000 euro.)

6. _____
   (We have 7.000 euro.)

To ask how much something costs **in italiano,** one asks — **Quanto** *(kwahn-toh)* **costa?** *(koh-stah)*

Now you try it. _____
   (How much does that cost?)

Answer the following questions based on the numbers in parentheses.

7. **Quanto costa?** *(kwahn-toh) (koh-stah)* **Costa** *(koh-stah)* (it) costs _____ (7) **euro.** *(eh-oo-roh)*

8. **Quanto costa il libro?** *(lee-broh)* book **Il libro costa** _____ (6) **euro.**

9. **Quanto costa il film?** *(feelm)* **Il film costa** _____ (4) **euro.**

10. **Quanto costa la cartolina?** *(kar-toh-lee-nah)* postcard **La cartolina costa** _____ (2) **euro.**

21

8   Oggi, Domani e Ieri
(oh-jee)   *(doh-mah-nee)*   *(ee-eh-ree)*
today   tomorrow   and   yesterday

(kah-len-dah-ree-oh)
Il calendario
calendar

_____

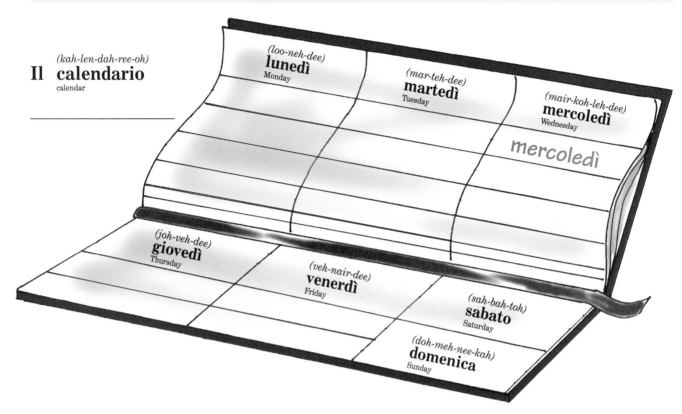

(loo-neh-dee)
lunedì
Monday

(mar-teh-dee)
martedì
Tuesday

(mair-koh-leh-dee)
mercoledì
Wednesday

mercoledì

(joh-veh-dee)
giovedì
Thursday

(veh-nair-dee)
venerdì
Friday

(sah-bah-toh)
sabato
Saturday

(doh-meh-nee-kah)
domenica
Sunday

(kah-len-dah-ree-oh)
Learn the days of the week by writing them in **il calendario** above **e** then move on to the

(kwaht-troh)   *(jor-noh)*
quattro parts to each **giorno.**
four   day

(maht-tee-nah)
la mattina
morning

(poh-meh-ree-joh)
il pomeriggio
afternoon

(seh-rah)
la sera
evening

(noht-teh)
la notte
night

_____ _____ _____ _____

☐ **la famiglia** *(fah-meel-yah)*............... family	**f**	_____
☐ **famoso** *(fah-moh-zoh)*.................... famous		_____
☐ **la farmacia** *(far-mah-chee-ah)* .... pharmacy, drugstore		_____
☐ **il favore** *(fah-voh-reh)*................... favor		_____
– **per favore** *(pair)(fah-voh-reh)* .... please		_____

È *(mohl-toh)* **molto** *(eem-por-tahn-teh)* **importante** to know the days of the week **e** the various parts of the day as well as
it is   very   important

these **tre parole.**

(ee-eh-ree)
ieri

(oh-jee)
oggi

(doh-mah-nee)
domani

(loo-neh-dee)
lunedì
Monday

(mar-teh-dee)
martedì
Tuesday

(mair-koh-leh-dee)
mercoledì
Wednesday

(joh-veh-dee)
giovedì
Thursday

(veh-nair-dee)
venerdì
Friday

(sah-bah-toh)
sabato
Saturday

(doh-meh-nee-kah)
domenica
Sunday

(keh) *(jor-noh)* *(oh-jee)*
Che giorno è oggi?_____
what   day   is

(doh-mah-nee)
Che giorno è domani?_____

(eh-rah) *(ee-eh-ree)*
Che giorno era ieri? _____
was

(oh-jee)
Oggi è mercoledì, sì? So, _____
yes   (tomorrow)

è giovedì e _____ **era martedì. Gli Italiani** begin counting their
              (yesterday)   was   the Italians

(l-yee) *(ee-tahl-yah-nee)*

(set-tee-mah-nah)
settimana on Monday with **lunedì.** In Italian, the days of the **settimana** are not capitalized
week   week

(loo-neh-dee)   *(set-tee-mah-nah)*

as **in inglese.**

a.	Sunday morning	=	_____
b.	Friday morning	=	_____
c.	Saturday evening	=	_____
d.	Thursday afternoon	=	_____
e.	Thursday evening	=	_____
f.	yesterday evening	=	_____
g.	tomorrow afternoon	=	_____
h.	tomorrow evening	=	_____

_____ _____ **è il** *(kohn-chair-toh)* **concerto?**
(when) (when)   concert

_____ _____ **è?**
(who)   (who)   is it

23

Knowing the parts of **il giorno** *(jor-noh)* [day] will help you to learn the various **saluti italiani** *(sah-loo-tee)* *(ee-tahl-yah-nee)* [greetings] below.

Practice these every day until your trip.

(bwohn) *(jor-noh)*
buon giorno _____
good morning / good day

(bwoh-nah) *(seh-rah)*
buona sera _____
good   evening

(bwoh-nah) *(noht-teh)*
buona notte _____
good   night

(chow)
ciao _____
hi! / bye!

Take the next **quattro** *(kwah-troh)* [four] labels **e** stick them on the appropriate **cose** *(koh-zeh)* [things] in your **casa.** [house] Make sure you attach them to the correct items, as they are only **in italiano.** How about the bathroom mirror **per "buon giorno"?** *(pair)* *(bwohn)* *(jor-noh)* [for] **o** *(oh)* your alarm clock **per "buona notte"?** *(pair)* *(bwoh-nah)* *(noht-teh)* Let's not forget,

(koh-meh) *(stah)*
Come sta? _____
How are you

Now for some " **sì** " *(see)* [yes] or " **no** " *(no)* [no] questions –

Are your eyes **blu?** *(bloo)* _____   Are your shoes **marroni?** *(mar-roh-nee)* _____

Is your favorite color **rosso?** *(rohs-soh)* _____   Is today **sabato?** *(sah-bah-toh)* _____

Do you have a **cane?** *(kah-neh)* _____   Do you have a **gatto?** *(gaht-toh)* _____

You **è** about one-fourth of your way through this **libro** *(lee-broh)* [book] and it is a good time to quickly review

le parole you have learned before doing the crossword puzzle on the next **pagina.**

Buon divertimento e buona fortuna. *(bwohn)* *(dee-vair-tee-men-toh)* *(for-too-nah)*
have fun   good   luck

RISPOSTE TO THE CROSSWORD PUZZLE (PAROLE CROCIATE)

DOWN
1. venerdì
2. ieri
3. cugino/a
4. sedia
5. sabato
6. diciannove
7. pomeriggio
8. acqua
9. banca
10. cartolina
11. dove
13. ciao
14. che cos'è
15. insalata
16. venti
17. bianco
19. tendina
20. lampada
21. quattro
22. martedì
23. due
24. rosso
25. come

ACROSS
1. vorrei
2. cane
3. grigio
4. signore
5. nove
6. giardino
7. domenica
8. con
9. moneta
10. cinque
11. denaro
12. nero
13. giallo
14. chi
15. giorno
16. verde
17. Italia
18. orologio
19. tre
21. quanto
22. multicolore
23. sera
24. oggi
26. notte
27. ecco
28. abbiamo

CROSSWORD PUZZLE (PAROLE CROCIATE)

(kroh-chah-teh)

ACROSS

1. I would like
2. dog
3. gray
4. man
5. nine
6. garden
7. Sunday
8. with
9. coin
10. five
11. money
12. black
13. yellow
14. who
15. day
16. green
17. Italy
18. clock
19. three
21. how much
22. multi-colored
23. evening
24. today
26. night
27. here is / are
28. we have

DOWN

1. Friday
2. yesterday
3. cousin
4. chair
5. Saturday
6. nineteen
7. afternoon
8. water
9. bank
10. postcard
11. where
13. hi! / bye!
14. what is it (what thing is it)
15. salad
16. twenty
17. white
19. curtain
20. lamp
21. four
22. Tuesday
23. two
24. red
25. how

❐	**il filtro** *(feel-troh)*	filter	
❐	**finalmente** *(fee-nahl-men-teh)*	finally	
❐	**finito** *(fee-nee-toh)*	finished, ended	**f**
❐	**la fontana** *(fohn-tah-nah)*	fountain	
❐	**la forchetta** *(for-ket-tah)*	fork	

9

(een) *(dah)* *(soh-prah)*
In, da, sopra...
in   from   over

(preh-poh-zee-tsee-oh-nee)
Le preposizioni italiane (words like "in," "on," "through" and "next to") **sono** easy to
prepositions   are

learn, **e** they allow you to be precise **con** a minimum of effort. Instead of having to point **sei**
(seh-ee)

times at a piece of yummy pastry you would like, you can explain precisely which one you want

by saying **è** behind, in front of, next to **o** under the piece of pastry that the salesperson is
(eh)
it is

starting to pick up. Let's learn some of these **piccole parole.**
(peek-koh-leh)
little

(soht-toh)
sotto———————————————
under

(een)   *(nel-lah)*
in (also seen as **nel, nella**) ——————
into / in / to   in the

(soh-prah)
sopra ————————————————
over

(dah-vahn-tee) *(dah-vahn-tee)* *(ahl)*
davanti a / davanti al—————————
in front of in front of the

(frah) *(trah)*
fra / tra ——————————————
between

(dee-eh-troh)
dietro ———————————————
behind

(ahk-kahn-toh) *(ah)* *(ahk-kahn-toh)* *(ahl)*
accanto a / accanto al—————————
next to next to the

(dah)   *(dahl)* *(dahl-lah)*
da (also seen as **dal, dalla**) ——————
from   from the

(soo) *(sool)* *(sool-lah)*
su (sul, sulla)—————————————
on   on the

(pah-stah)
la pasta————————————————
pastry!

When followed by "the," many of these **piccole parole** join together with "the" and change their

forms slightly.

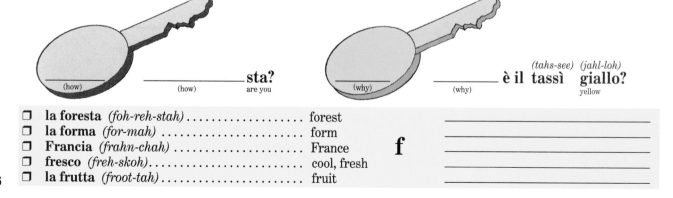

_____ _____ **sta?**
(how)   (how)   are you

_____ **è il tassì giallo?**
(why)   (why)   *(tahs-see) (jahl-loh)*
                            yellow

❑	**la foresta** *(foh-reh-stah)*	forest	
❑	**la forma** *(for-mah)*	form	
❑	**Francia** *(frahn-chah)*	France	**f**
❑	**fresco** *(freh-skoh)*	cool, fresh	
❑	**la frutta** *(froot-tah)*	fruit	

26

La pasta è _____ *(tah-voh-loh)* **tavolo.**
pastry (on + the) table

(kah-neh)
Il cane nero è _____ **il tavolo.**
dog (under) table

(meh-dee-koh) *(ahl-bair-goh)*
Il medico è _____ **buon albergo.**
doctor (in + the) hotel

Dov'è il medico? _____

(seen-yoh-reh)
Il signore è _____ **albergo.**
man (in front of + the)

Dov'è il signore? _____

(teh-leh-foh-noh) *(kwah-droh)*
Il telefono è _____ **quadro.**
telephone (next to + the) picture

Dov'è il telefono? _____

(ah-des-soh)
Adesso, fill in each blank on the picture below with the best possible one of these **piccole** *(peek-koh-leh)*
now little

parole. One of the many sights you might see could be **il Ponte Vecchio**. Do you recognize it
(pohn-teh) (vek-kee-oh)
old bridge in Florence

in the picture below?

_____
(over)

_____
(in)

_____
(behind)

_____
(under)

_____
(between)

_____
(in front of)

❐	**la galleria** *(gahl-leh-ree-ah)*	gallery, tunnel	_____
❐	**gennaio** *(jen-ny-oh)*	January	_____
❐	**gentile** *(jen-tee-leh)*	kind, gentle **g**	_____
❐	**la geografia** *(jeh-oh-grah-fee-ah)*	geography	_____
❐	**la giacca** *(jahk-kah)*	jacket	_____

10

(jen-ny-oh) *(feb-bry-oh)* *(mar-tsoh)*
Gennaio, Febbraio, Marzo
January   February   March

You have learned the days of **la settimana,** *(set-tee-mah-nah)* so now **è il momento** *(moh-men-toh)* to learn **i mesi** *(meh-zee)* **dell'anno** *(del-lahn-noh)*
week   it is moment   months of the year

e all the different kinds of **tempo.** *(tem-poh)*
weather

(jen-ny-oh)
gennaio
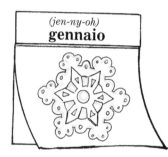

(feb-bry-oh)
febbraio

(mar-tsoh)
marzo

(ah-pree-leh)
aprile

(mah-joh)
maggio

(joon-yoh)
giugno

(lool-yoh)
luglio

(ah-goh-stoh)
agosto

(set-tem-breh)
settembre

(oht-toh-breh)
ottobre

(noh-vem-breh)
novembre

(dee-chem-breh)
dicembre

When someone asks, " <u>**Che tempo fa oggi?**</u> " you have a variety of answers. Let's learn
what is the weather making today
(keh)   *(fah)* *(oh-jee)*

them but first, does this sound familiar?

(ah) *(set-tem-breh)* *(ah-pree-leh)* *(joon-yoh)* *(noh-vem-breh)*
Trenta giorni ha settembre, aprile, giugno e novembre . . .
has

☐ **il giardino** *(jar-dee-noh)* . . . . garden
☐ **giugno** *(joon-yoh)* . . . . June
☐ **il governo** *(goh-vair-noh)* . . . . government   **g**
☐ **grande** *(grahn-deh)* . . . . big, large, grand
☐ **la guida** *(gwee-dah)* . . . . guide

(keh) *(oh-jee)*
Che tempo fa oggi? _____
what   today

(neh-vee-kah)
Nevica in gennaio. _____
it snows   in

(ahn-keh)
Nevica anche in febbraio. _____
also

(pee-oh-veh)
Piove in marzo. _____
it rains

(ahn-keh)
Piove anche in aprile. _____
also

(cheh) *(ven-toh)* *(mah-joh)*
C'è vento in maggio. _____
it's   windy

(cheh) *(soh-leh)* *(joon-yoh)*
C'è sole in giugno. _____
there is sun

(lool-yoh)
C'è sole anche in luglio. _____

(fah) *(kahl-doh)*
Fa caldo in agosto. _____
it makes warm

Fa bello in settembre. _____
nice

(freh-skoh)
Fa fresco in ottobre. _____
cool

(broot-toh)
Fa brutto in novembre. _____
bad

(fred-doh)
Fa freddo in dicembre. _____
cold

(keh)
Che tempo fa in febbraio? _____

Che tempo fa in aprile? _____

Che tempo fa in maggio? _____

Che tempo fa in settembre? _____

❐ **incantevole** *(een-kahn-teh-voh-leh)* . . . . enchanting, charming _____
❐ **indispensabile** *(een-dee-spen-sah-bee-leh)* . . . indispensable _____
❐ **l'individuo** *(leen-dee-vee-doo-oh)* . . . . individual (person) **i** _____
❐ **l'industria** *(leen-doo-stree-ah)* . . . . industry _____
❐ **industrioso** *(een-doo-stree-oh-zoh)* . . . . industrious _____

29

Adesso for **le** *(stah-joh-nee)* **stagioni** *(del-lahn-noh)* **dell'anno...**
of the   year

(leen-vair-noh)
l'inverno
winter

(leh-stah-teh)
l'estate
summer

(lah-oo-toon-noh)
l'autunno
autumn

(pree-mah-veh-rah)
la primavera
spring

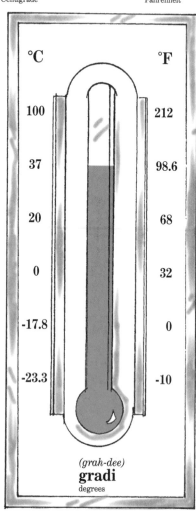

(chen-tee-grah-doh)
Centigrado
Centigrade

(fah-ren-heit)
Fahrenheit
Fahrenheit

°C		°F
100		212
37		98.6
20		68
0		32
-17.8		0
-23.3		-10

(grah-dee)
gradi
degrees

At this point, **è una buona idea** to familiarize
(eh) *(bwoh-nah)* *(ee-deh-ah)*
good

yourself **con le temperature europee.**
(tem-peh-rah-too-reh) *(eh-oo-roh-peh-eh)*
temperatures   European

Carefully study **il termometro** because **le**
(tair-moh-meh-troh)

temperature in Europa are calculated on the
(ee-oo-roh-pah)

basis of Centigrade (not Fahrenheit).

To convert °F to °C, subtract 32 and multiply by 0.55.

$$98.6\,°F - 32 = 66.6 \times 0.55 = 37\,°C$$

To convert °C to °F, multiply by 1.8 and add 32.

$$37\,°C \times 1.8 = 66.6 + 32 = 98.6\,°F$$

What is normal body temperature in **Centigrado?**

What is the freezing point in **Centigrado?**

11   *(fah-meel-yah)*   *(fah-meh)*   *(feh-deh)*
Famiglia, Fame, e Fede
family   hunger   faith

Just as we have the three "R's" **in inglese, in italiano** there are the three **"F's"** (**famiglia,**

(fah-meel-yah)

(fah-meh)   *(feh-deh)*   *(vee-tah)*   *(ee-tahl-yah-nah)*

fame e fede) which help us to understand some of the basics of **la vita italiana.**   Study the
life   Italian

family tree below.

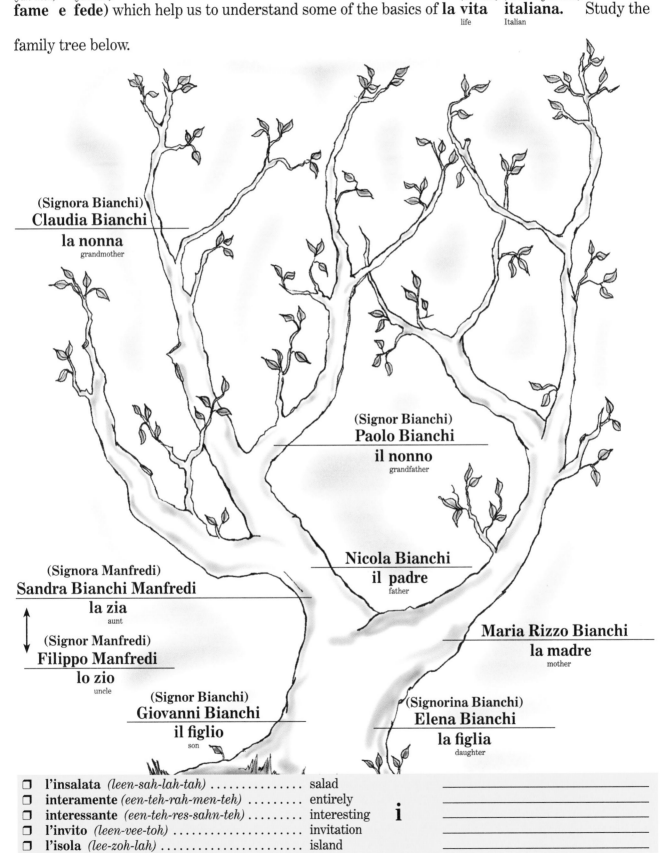

(Signora Bianchi)
Claudia Bianchi
la nonna
grandmother

(Signor Bianchi)
Paolo Bianchi
il nonno
grandfather

Nicola Bianchi
il padre
father

(Signora Manfredi)
Sandra Bianchi Manfredi
la zia
aunt

(Signor Manfredi)
Filippo Manfredi
lo zio
uncle

Maria Rizzo Bianchi
la madre
mother

(Signor Bianchi)
Giovanni Bianchi
il figlio
son

(Signorina Bianchi)
Elena Bianchi
la figlia
daughter

❏ **l'insalata** *(leen-sah-lah-tah)* . . . . salad		
❏ **interamente** *(een-teh-rah-men-teh)* . . . . entirely		
❏ **interessante** *(een-teh-res-sahn-teh)* . . . . interesting	**i**	
❏ **l'invito** *(leen-vee-toh)* . . . . invitation		
❏ **l'isola** *(lee-zoh-lah)* . . . . island		

31

Let's learn how to identify **la famiglia** *(fah-meel-yah)* by **nome** *(noh-meh)*. Study the following **esempi** *(eh-zem-pee)* carefully.

family — name — examples

Come si chiama? *(koh-meh)(see)(kee-ah-mah)* _____

what is your name / how are you called

Mi chiamo *(mee)(kee-ah-moh)* _____

my name is / I am called _____ (your name)

i genitori *(jeh-nee-toh-ree)*

parents

il padre *(pah-dreh)* _____

father

Come si chiama il padre? *(kee-ah-mah)* _____

how — is called — the father

la madre *(mah-dreh)* _____

mother

Come si chiama la madre? _____

how — is called — mother

i figli *(feel-yee)*

children

il figlio e la figlia *(feel-yoh)(feel-yah)* = **fratello e sorella** *(frah-tel-loh)(soh-rel-lah)*

brother — sister

il figlio *(feel-yoh)* _____

son

Come si chiama il figlio? *(kee-ah-mah)(feel-yoh)* _____

son

la figlia *(feel-yah)* _____

daughter

Come si chiama la figlia? *(see)(feel-yah)* _____

daughter

i parenti *(pah-ren-tee)*

relatives

il nonno *(nohn-noh)* _____

grandfather

Come si chiama il nonno? *(koh-meh)* _____

grandfather

la nonna *(nohn-nah)* _____

grandmother

Come si chiama la nonna? *(kee-ah-mah)* _____

grandmother

Now you ask —

_____

(How are you called? / What is your name?)

And answer —

_____

(My name is . . .)

❏	**il lago** *(lah-goh)*	lake		_____
❏	**largo** *(lar-goh)*	wide, broad		_____
❏	**il legume** *(leh-goo-meh)*	vegetable	**l**	_____
❏	**la lettera** *(let-teh-rah)*	letter		_____
❏	**la lezione** *(leh-tsee-oh-neh)*	lesson, lecture		_____

La Cucina

(koo-chee-nah)

kitchen

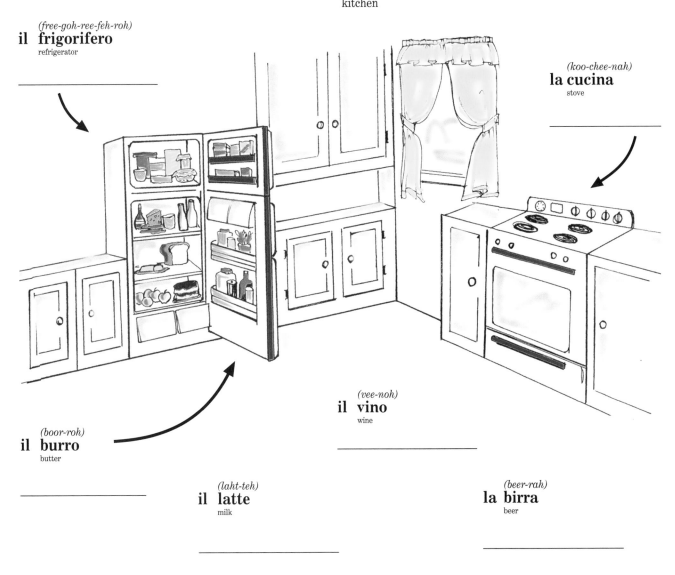

il frigorifero
(free-goh-ree-feh-roh)
refrigerator

la cucina
(koo-chee-nah)
stove

il burro
(boor-roh)
butter

il vino
(vee-noh)
wine

il latte
(laht-teh)
milk

la birra
(beer-rah)
beer

Answer these questions aloud.

Dov'è la birra? *(beer-rah)* beer .... **La birra è nel frigorifero.** *(free-goh-ree-feh-roh)* in the

Dov'è il latte? milk

Dov'è il vino ? wine

Dov'è il burro? butter

Adesso apra *(ah-prah)* open your **libro** *(lee-broh)* book to the **pagina con** the labels **e** remove the next group of labels **e** proceed to label all these **cose** *(koh-zeh)* things in your **cucina.** *(koo-chee-nah)* kitchen

☐ **libero** *(lee-beh-roh)*	free, liberated	
☐ **la lingua** *(leen-gwah)*	language	
☐ **la lista** *(lee-stah)*	list	**l**
☐ **la lotteria** *(loht-teh-ree-ah)*	lottery	
☐ **lungo** *(loon-goh)*	long	

33

(sah-leh)
il sale
salt

(peh-peh)
il pepe
pepper

(beek-kee-eh-reh) *(vee-noh)*
il bicchiere di vino
wine glass

(beek-kee-eh-reh)
il bicchiere
glass

(fee-oh-reh)
il fiore
flower

(tah-tsah)
la tazza
cup

(jor-nah-leh)
il giornale
newspaper

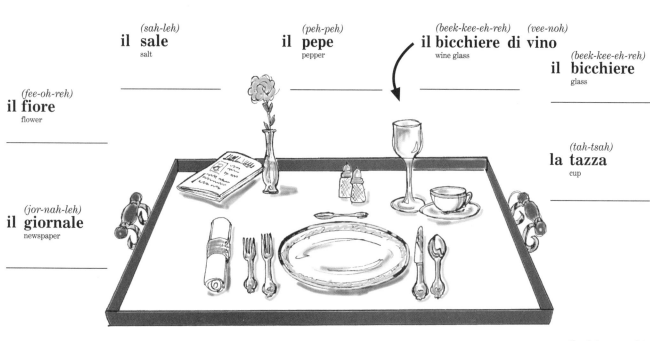

(toh-vahl-yoh-loh)
il tovagliolo
napkin

(kook-kee-eye-oh)
il cucchiaio
spoon

(for-ket-tah)
la forchetta
fork

(pee-aht-toh)
il piatto
plate

(kohl-tel-loh)
il coltello
knife

E more . . .

(lar-mah-dee-et-toh)
l'armadietto
cupboard

(teh)
il tè _____
tea

(doh-veh)
Dov'è il tè?

(nel-lar-mah-dee-et-toh)
Il tè è nell'armadietto.

(kahf-feh)
il caffè _____
coffee

Dov'è il caffè?

(pah-neh)
il pane _____
bread

Dov'è il pane?

Don't forget to label all these things and do not forget to use every

opportunity to say these **parole** out loud. **È molto importante.**
(eem-por-tahn-teh)
very

(preh-goh) **prego**	*(frahn-koh-bohl-loh)* **il francobollo**	*(pet-tee-neh)* **il pettine**	*(short)* **gli short**
(let-toh) **il letto**	*(kar-toh-lee-nah)* **la cartolina**	*(kahp-poht-toh)* **il cappotto**	*(mahl-yet-tah)* **la maglietta**
(koo-shee-noh) **il cuscino**	*(pahs-sah-por-toh)* **il passaporto**	*(lohm-brel-loh)* **l'ombrello**	*(moo-tahn-deh)* **le mutande**
(koh-pair-tah) **la coperta**	*(beel-yet-toh)* **il biglietto**	*(leem-pair-meh-ah-bee-leh)* **l'impermeabile**	*(kah-noht-tee-eh-rah)* **la canottiera**
(zvel-yah) **la sveglia**	*(vah-lee-jah)* **la valigia**	*(gwahn-tee)* **i guanti**	*(veh-stee-toh)* **il vestito**
(spek-kee-oh) **lo specchio**	*(bor-sah)* **la borsa**	*(kahp-pel-loh)* **il cappello**	*(kah-mee-chet-tah)* **la camicetta**
(lah-vahn-dee-noh) **il lavandino**	*(por-tah-fohl-yoh)* **il portafoglio**	*(kahp-pel-loh)* **il cappello**	*(gohn-nah)* **la gonna**
(ah-shoo-gah-mah-nee) **i asciugamani**	*(deh-nah-roh)* **il denaro**	*(stee-vah-lee)* **gli stivali**	*(gohl-fee-noh)* **il golfino**
(vee-chee) **il W.C.**	*(kar-teh)* *(kreh-dee-toh)* **le carte di credito**	*(skar-peh)* **le scarpe**	*(soht-toh-veh-steh)* **la sottoveste**
(doh-chah) **la doccia**	*(trah-vel)* *(check)* **i travel check**	*(skar-peh)* *(ten-nees)* **le scarpe da tennis**	*(reh-jee-pet-toh)* **il reggipetto**
(mah-tee-tah) **la matita**	*(mahk-kee-nah)* *(foh-toh-grah-fee-kah)* **la macchina fotografica**	*(lah-bee-toh)* **l'abito**	*(moo-tahn-dee-neh)* **le mutandine**
(teh-leh-vee-zee-oh-neh) **il televisione**	*(rool-lee-noh)* **il rullino**	*(krah-vaht-tah)* **la cravatta**	*(kahl-tsee-nee)* **i calzini**
(pen-nah) **la penna**	*(koh-stoo-meh)* *(bahn-yoh)* **il costume da bagno**	*(kah-mee-chah)* **la camicia**	*(kahl-tseh)* **le calze**
(ree-vee-stah) **la rivista**	*(sahn-dah-lee)* **i sandali**	*(fah-tsoh-let-toh)* **il fazzoletto**	*(pee-jah-mah)* **il pigiama**
(lee-broh) **il libro**	*(ohk-kee-ah-lee)* *(soh-leh)* **gli occhiali da sole**	*(jahk-kah)* **la giacca**	*(kah-mee-chah)* *(noht-teh)* **la camicia da notte**
(kohm-pyoo-tair) **il computer**	*(spah-tsoh-lee-noh)* *(den-tee)* **lo spazzolino da denti**	*(pahn-tah-loh-nee)* **i pantaloni**	*(lahk-kahp-pah-toy-oh)* **l'accappatoio**
(ohk-kee-ah-lee) **gli occhiali**	*(den-tee-free-choh)* **il dentifricio**	*(jeans)* **i jeans**	*(pahn-toh-foh-leh)* **le pantofole**
(kar-tah) **la carta**	*(sah-poh-neh)* **il sapone**	*(ven-goh)* *(dahl-yee)* *(stah-tee)* *(oo-nee-tee)* **Vengo dagli Stati Uniti.**	
(cheh-stee-noh) **il cestino**	*(rah-zoy-oh)* **il rasoio**	*(vor-reh-ee)* *(eem-pah-rah-reh)* *(lee-tahl-yah-noh)* **Vorrei imparare l'italiano.**	
(let-teh-rah) **la lettera**	*(deh-oh-doh-rahn-teh)* **il deodorante**	*(mee)* *(kee-ah-moh)* **Mi chiamo _____.**	

PLUS...

This book includes a number of other innovative features unique to the *"10 minutes a day*®*"* series. At the back of this book you will find twelve pages of flash cards. Cut them out and flip through them at least once a day.

On pages 116, 117 and 118 you will find a beverage guide and a menu guide. Don't wait until your trip to use them. Clip out the menu guide and use it tonight at the dinner table. Take them both with you the next time you dine at your favorite Italian restaurant.

By using the special features in this book, you will be speaking Italian before you know it.

(bwohn)   *(dee-vair-tee-men-toh)*
Buon divertimento!
have fun

(kee-eh-zah)
La Chiesa
church

In Italia there is not the wide variety of *(reh-lee-joh-nee)* **religioni** that *(ahb-bee-ah-moh)* **abbiamo** *(kwee)* **qui in**
religions   we have   here

(ah-meh-ree-kah) **America.** A person **è** *(jeh-neh-rahl-men-teh)* **generalmente** one of the following.
      generally

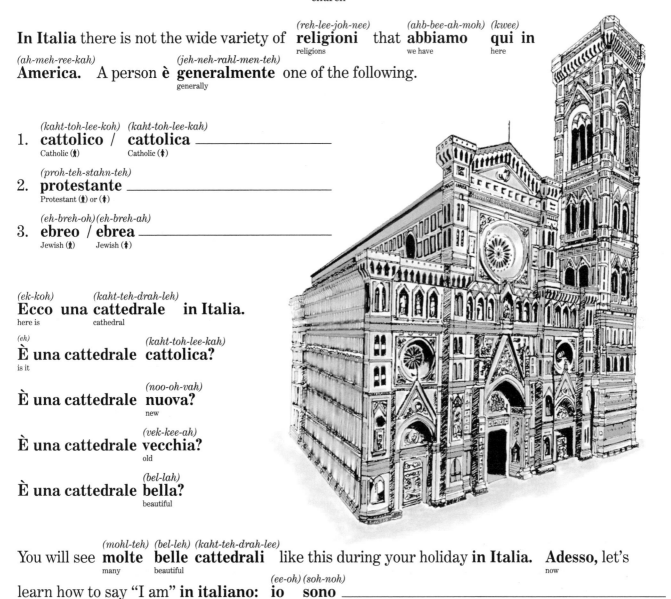

1. *(kaht-toh-lee-koh)* *(kaht-toh-lee-kah)*
   cattolico / cattolica _____
   Catholic (♂)   Catholic (♀)

2. *(proh-teh-stahn-teh)*
   protestante _____
   Protestant (♂) or (♀)

3. *(eh-breh-oh)(eh-breh-ah)*
   ebreo / ebrea _____
   Jewish (♂)   Jewish (♀)

(ek-koh) *(kaht-teh-drah-leh)*
Ecco una cattedrale in Italia.
here is   cathedral

(eh)
È una cattedrale *(kaht-toh-lee-kah)* **cattolica?**
is it

È una cattedrale *(noo-oh-vah)* **nuova?**
      new

È una cattedrale *(vek-kee-ah)* **vecchia?**
      old

È una cattedrale *(bel-lah)* **bella?**
      beautiful

(mohl-teh) (bel-leh) (kaht-teh-drah-lee)
You will see **molte belle cattedrali** like this during your holiday **in Italia.** **Adesso,** let's
    many   beautiful   now

learn how to say "I am" **in italiano:** *(ee-oh) (soh-noh)* **io sono** _____
      I   am

To make an adjective feminine **in italiano,** you usually change the **"o"** at the end to an **"a."**

Adjectives that end in **"e"** can be either masculine or feminine. Test yourself — write each

sentence on the next page for more practice. Add your own personal variations as well.

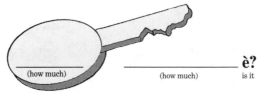

_____ _____ **è?**
(how much)   (how much)   is it

☐	**il medico** *(meh-dee-koh)*	doctor, physician	_____
☐	**la memoria** *(meh-moh-ree-ah)*	memory	_____
☐	**meno** *(meh-noh)*	minus, less **m**	_____
☐	**meraviglioso** *(meh-rah-veel-yoh-zoh)*	marvelous	_____
☐	**il mercato** *(mair-kah-toh)*	market	_____

(ee-oh) (soh-noh) (kaht-toh-lee-koh) **Io sono cattolico.** ____ I am Catholic (♂)	*(proh-teh-stahn-teh)* **Io sono protestante.** ____
(eh-breh-oh) **Io sono ebreo.** ____ Jewish (♂)	*(ah-meh-ree-kah-noh)* **Io sono americano.** ____ American (♂)
(eh-oo-roh-pah) **Io sono in Europa.** ____ Europe	*(kah-nah-deh-zeh)* **Io sono canadese.** ____ Canadian
(kee-eh-zah) **Io sono nella chiesa.** ____ I am in the church	**Io sono in Italia.** ____
(kaht-toh-lee-kah) **Io sono cattolica.** ____ Catholic (♀)	*(see-chee-lee-ah)* **Io sono in Sicilia.** ____ Sicily
(nel-lahl-bair-goh) **Io sono nell'albergo.** ____ in the hotel	*(ree-stoh-rahn-teh)* **Io sono nel ristorante.** ____ in the
Io sono nella cucina. ____ in the kitchen	*(stahn-koh)* **Io sono stanco.** ____ tired

To negate any of these statements, simply add *(nohn)* "**non**" (not / no) before the verb.

Io *(nohn)* **non** (not) **sono protestante.** ____

Io non (not) **sono** *(stahn-koh)* **stanco** (tired)**.** ____

Go through and drill these sentences again but with "**non.**"

Adesso, take a piece of paper. Our *(fah-meel-yah)* **famiglia** from earlier had a reunion. Identify everyone below by writing **la parola italiana** *(kor-ret-tah)* **corretta** (correct) for each person — **la madre, lo zio** and so on. Don't forget **il** *(kah-neh)* **cane!**

❐ **il metallo** *(meh-tahl-loh)*	metal	**m**	____
❐ **il metro** *(meh-troh)*	meter		____
❐ **milione** *(meel-yoh-neh)*	million		____
❐ **la misura** *(mee-zoo-rah)*	measure, size		____
❐ **la moda** *(moh-dah)*	style, fashion		____

(eem-pah-rah-reh)
Imparare!
to learn

You have already used **due** *(doo-eh)* very important verbs: **vorrei** *(vor-reh-ee)* and **ho** *(oh)*. Although you might be able
I would like   I have

to get by with only these verbs, let's assume you want to do better. First,

How do you say   "**I**"   in italiano?_____

How do you say   "**we**"   in italiano?_____

Compare these **due** charts very carefully **e** learn these **sei** *(seh-ee)* **parole** now.
two   six

I = **io** *(ee-oh)* _____	we = **noi** *(noy)* _____
he = **lui** *(loo-ee)* _____	you = **Lei** *(leh-ee)* _____
she = **lei** *(leh-ee)* _____	they = **loro** *(loh-roh)* _____

Not too hard, is it? Draw lines between the matching **parole** **inglesi** *(een-gleh-zee)* **e** **italiane** *(ee-tahl-yah-neh)* below to

see if you can keep these **parole** straight in your mind.

noi *(noy)*   I

loro   you

lei *(leh-ee)*   they

Lei   he

io   we

lui *(loo-ee)*   she

Note: "**Lei**" with a capital "L" means "you," and "**lei**" with a lower case "l" means "she."

❏	**il motore** *(moh-toh-reh)*	motor, engine	_____
❏	**il momento** *(moh-men-toh)*	moment	_____
	— **Un momento!**	Just a moment! **m**	_____
❏	**la montagna** *(mohn-tahn-yah)*	mountain	_____
❏	**il museo** *(moo-zeh-oh)*	museum	_____

Adesso close **il libro e** write out both columns of this practice on a piece of **carta.** *(kar-tah)* paper How did **Lei** *(leh-ee)* do? **Bene o male?** *(beh-neh)* *(mah-leh)* good or bad **Adesso** that **Lei** you know these **parole, Lei** you can say almost anything

in italiano with one basic formula: the "plug-in" formula.

To demonstrate, let's take **sei** *(seh-ee)* six basic **e** practical verbs **e** see how the "plug-in" formula works.

Write the verbs in the blanks after **Lei** have practiced saying them out loud many times.

(par-lah-reh)
parlare _____
to speak

(ah-bee-tah-reh)
abitare _____
to live, to reside

(pren-deh-reh)
prendere _____
to take

(kohm-prah-reh)
comprare _____
to buy

(eem-pah-rah-reh)
imparare _____
to learn

(kee-ah-mar-see)
chiamarsi _____
to be called

Besides the familiar words already circled, can **Lei** find four of the above verbs in the puzzle

below? When **Lei** find them, write them in the blanks to the right.

A	C	O	H	A	F	I	J	Y	T	P
B	O	C	E	C	H	E	A	R	E	A
I	M	P	A	R	A	R	E	L	N	R
T	P	R	E	N	D	C	O	M	E	L
A	R	M	E	C	U	E	R	E	R	A
R	A	D	U	Y	H	T	S	E	I	R
E	R	N	O	R	D	I	N	A	R	E
Y	E	G	T	S	E	D	D	O	V	E

1. _____

2. _____

3. _____

4. _____

5. _____

□ **la musica** *(moo-zee-kah)* .... music
□ **nativo** *(nah-tee-voh)* .... native
□ **naturale** *(nah-too-rah-leh)*............. natural
□ **la nazione** *(nah-tsee-oh-neh)*............ nation, country
□ **necessario** *(neh-ches-sah-ree-oh)* .... necessary

m _____

n _____

40

Study the following patterns carefully.

io *(ee-oh)*	**parlo**	=	I *speak*
	(ah-bee-toh) **abito**	=	I *live / reside*
	prendo	=	I *take*
	(kohm-proh) **compro**	=	I *buy*
	imparo	=	I *learn*
io	*(mee) (kee-ah-moh)* **mi chiamo**	=	I *am called /* *my name is*

noi *(noy)*	**parliamo**	=	we *speak*
	(ah-bee-tee-ah-moh) **abitiamo**	=	we *live / reside*
	prendiamo	=	we *take*
	(kohm-pree-ah-moh) **compriamo**	=	we *buy*
	impariamo	=	we *learn*
noi	*(chee)* **ci chiamiamo**	=	we *are called /* *our name is*

Note: • With all these verbs, the first thing you do is drop the final **"are," "ere,"** or **"ire"**

from the basic verb form or stem.

• With **"io,"** add **"o"** to the basic verb form.

• With **"noi,"** add **"iamo."**

(kee-ah-mar-see)
• **Chiamarsi** is a bit different, so take a few extra minutes to learn it.

Some verbs just will not conform to the pattern! But don't worry. Speak slowly **e** clearly, **e**

you will be perfectly understood whether you say **"io parlo"** or **"io parla."** Italian speakers

will be delighted that you have taken the time to learn their language.

Note: • Italian has four separate ways of saying "you."

• **"Lei"** will be used throughout this book and will be appropriate for most

situations. **"Lei"** refers to one person in a formal sense.

(too) you
• **"Tu"** is usually reserved for family members and very close friends.
you (singular)

(voy) *(too)*
• **"Voi"** is the plural of **"tu."**
you (plural)

(leh-ee)
• **"Loro"** is the plural of **"Lei."**
you (plural)

❏	**il nome** *(noh-meh)*	name		_____
❏	**nord** *(nord)*	north		_____
❏	**normale** *(nor-mah-leh)*	normal	**n**	_____
❏	**la notizia** *(noh-tee-tsee-ah)*	news, notice		_____
❏	**nuovo** *(noo-oh-voh)*	new		_____

Here's your next group of patterns.

(leh-ee) **Lei** you *(loo-ee)* **lui** he *(leh-ee)* **lei** she }	**parl<u>a</u>** = you, he, she *speak(s)*	
	abit<u>a</u> = you, he, she *live(s)/reside(s)*	
	prend<u>e</u> = you, he, she *take(s)*	
	compr<u>a</u> = you, he, she *buy(s)*	
	impar<u>a</u> = you, he, she *learn(s)*	
	(kee-ah-mah) **si chiam<u>a</u>** = your *name is* his/her *name is*	

(loh-roh) **loro** they }	**parl<u>ano</u>** = they *speak*	
	abit<u>ano</u> = they *live/reside*	
	prend<u>ono</u> = they *take*	
	compr<u>ano</u> = they *buy*	
	impar<u>ano</u> = they *learn*	
	si chiam<u>ano</u> = their *name is*	

Note:
- Again drop the final **"are," "ere,"** or **"ire"** from the basic verb form or stem.
- With **"Lei,"** you **"lui"** and **"lei,"** she add **"a"** if the original ending was **"are,"** and **"e"** for all others.
- With **"loro,"** simply add **"ano"** to the stem if the original ending was **"are,"** and **"ono"** for all others.

Ecco sei more verbs.
here are six

(veh-nee-reh) **venire** to come _____

(ah-veh-reh) **avere** to have _____

(dee-reh) **dire** to say

(ahn-dah-reh) **andare** to go _____

(ah-veh-reh) (bee-zohn-yoh) (dee) **avere bisogno di** to have need of _____

(vor-reh-ee) **vorrei** (I) would like

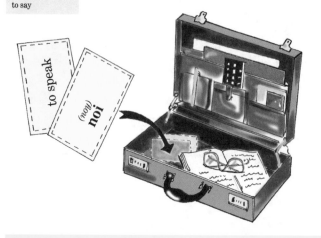

At the back of **il libro, Lei** will find twelve

(pah-jee-neh) **pagine** of flash cards to help you learn these
pages

(noo-oh-veh) **parole nuove.** Cut them out; carry them in
new

your briefcase, purse, pocket **o** knapsack; **e**
or

review them whenever **Lei** have a free moment.

☐ **l'occasione** *(lohk-kah-zee-oh-neh)* . . . . occasion, opportunity _____
☐ **occupato** *(ohk-koo-pah-toh)* . . . . occupied, busy _____
☐ **l'odore** *(loh-doh-reh)* . . . . odor (smell) **o** _____
☐ **l'oggetto** *(loh-jet-toh)* . . . . object _____
☐ **l'ombrello** *(lohm-brel-loh)* . . . . umbrella _____

Adesso, it is your turn to practice what **Lei** have learned. Fill in the following blanks with the correct form of the verb. Each time **Lei** write out the sentence, be sure to say it aloud.

(par-lah-reh)
parlare
to speak

Buon giorno!

Io _____ *(ee-tahl-yah-noh)* **italiano.**

Lei _____ *(een-gleh-zeh)* **inglese.**
English

Lui _____ *(frahn-cheh-zeh)* **francese.**
Lei (she) French

Noi _____ *(teh-deh-skoh)* **tedesco.**
German

Loro _____ *(spahn-yoh-loh)* **spagnolo.**
Spanish

(pren-deh-reh)
prendere
to take

Io _____ *(treh-noh)* **il treno.**
train

Lei _____ **la moto.**

Lui _____ *(bee-chee)* **la bici.**
Lei (she) bicycle

Noi _____ **l'autobus.**

Loro _____ **il treno per Venezia.**
Venice

(ah-bee-tah-reh)
abitare
to live, to reside

Io _____ **in Italia.**

Lei _____ **in America.**

Lui _____ *(eh-oo-roh-pah)* **in Europa.**
Lei (she)

Noi _____ *(een-gheel-tair-rah)* **in Inghilterra.**
England

Loro _____ *(frahn-chah)* **in Francia.**
France

(kohm-prah-reh)
comprare
to buy

Io _____ *(lee-broh)* **un libro.**

Lei _____ *(een-sah-lah-tah)* **un' insalata.**

Lui _____ *(mahk-kee-nah)* **una macchina.**
Lei (she) car

Noi _____ *(frahn-koh-bohl-lee)* **otto francobolli.**
stamps

Loro _____ *(beer-reh)* **due birre.**
beers

(eem-pah-rah-reh)
imparare
to learn

Io _____ **l'italiano.**

Lei _____ *(spahn-yoh-loh)* **lo spagnolo.**

Lui _____ **il tedesco.**
Lei (she) German

Noi _____ *(frahn-cheh-zeh)* **il francese.**
French

Loro _____ *(chee-neh-zeh)* **il cinese.**
Chinese

(kee-ah-mar-see)
chiamarsi
to be called

Mi chiamo Elena.

Io _mi chiamo/_____ **Nicola.**

Lei _____ **Giovanni.**

Lui _____ **Martini.**
Lei (she)

Noi _____ **Rizzo.**

Loro _si chiamano/_____ **Rossi.**

❏	**l'opera** *(loh-peh-rah)*	opera	_____
❏	**l'ora** *(loh-rah)*	hour, time	_____
❏	**ordinario** *(or-dee-nah-ree-oh)*	ordinary	**O** _____
❏	**l'ospedale** *(loh-speh-dah-leh)*	hospital	_____
❏	**ovest** *(oh-vest)*	west	_____

43

Now take a break, walk around the room, take a deep breath **e** do the next **sei** verbs.

(veh-nee-reh)
venire
to come

Io _vengo/_ *(dahl) (ree-stoh-rahn-teh)* **dal ristorante.**

Lei _viene/_ *(dahl-loof-fee-choh)* **dall'ufficio.**
office

Lui _____ **dalla banca.**
Lei (she)

Noi _veniamo/_ **dall'albergo.**

Loro _vengono/_ *(roh-mah)* **da Roma.**
Rome

(ahn-dah-reh)
andare
to go

Io _vado/_ **in Italia.**

Lei _va/_ *(frahn-chah)* **in Francia.**

Lui _____ *(spahn-yah)* **in Spagna.**
Lei (she)

Noi _andiamo/_ *(jair-mahn-yah)* **in Germania.**

Loro _vanno/_ *(por-toh-gahl-loh)* **in Portogallo.**
Portugal

(vor-reh-ee)
vorrei
(I) would like

Io _____ *(beek-kee-eh-reh) (vee-noh)* **un bicchiere di vino.**
glass   wine

Lei _vorrebbe/_ **un bicchiere di vino** *(rohs-soh)* **rosso.**
red

Lui _____ **un bicchiere di vino** *(bee-ahn-koh)* **bianco.**
Lei (she)   white

Noi _vorremmo/_ *(beek-kee-eh-ree)* **tre bicchieri di vino.**

Loro _vorrebbero/_ *(beer-reh)* **due birre.**
beers

(dee-reh)
dire
to say

Io _dico/_ *(bwohn) (jor-noh)* **"buon giorno."**

Lei _dice/_ **"sì."**

Lui _____ **"no."**
Lei (she)

Noi _diciamo/_ *(chow)* **"ciao."**

Loro non _dicono/_ *(nee-en-teh)* **niente.**
nothing

(ah-veh-reh)
avere
to have

Io _ho/_ *(ven-tee) (eh-oo-roh)* **venti euro.**

Lei _ha/_ *(tren-tah)* **trenta euro.**

Lui _____ *(oht-tahn-tah)* **ottanta euro.**
Lei (she)

Noi _abbiamo/_ *(chen-toh)* **cento euro.**

Loro _hanno/_ *(meel-leh)* **mille euro.**

(ah-veh-reh) (bee-zohn-yoh) (dee)
avere bisogno di
have   need   of / to need

Io _____ *(kah-meh-rah)* **una camera.**
room

Lei _____ *(dah-kwah)* **un bicchiere d'acqua.**

Lui _____ **un libro.**
Lei (she)

Noi _____ *(kah-meh-reh)* **quattro camere.**
rooms

Loro _____ **ottomila lire.**

❏	**il pacco** *(pahk-koh)*	package	
❏	**il paio** *(pie-yoh)*	pair	
	— un paio di scarpe	a pair of shoes	**p**
❏	**il palazzo** *(pah-lah-tsoh)*	palace, building	
❏	**i pantaloni** *(pahn-tah-loh-nee)*	pants, trousers	

Sì, it is hard to get used to all those **parole nuove.** Just keep practicing **e** before **Lei** know
yes

it, **Lei** will be using them naturally. **Adesso** is a perfect time to turn to the back of this **libro,**

clip out your verb flash cards **e** start flashing. Don't skip over your free **parole** either. Check

(eem-pah-rah)
them off in the box provided as **Lei impara** veach one. See if **Lei** can fill in the blanks
learn

below. **Le risposte corrette** are at the bottom of **la pagina.**
page

1. _____
(I speak Italian.)

2. _____
(We learn Italian.)

3. _____
(She needs 500 euro.)

4. _____
(He comes from the hotel.)

5. _____
(They live in Canada.)

6. _____
(You buy a book.)

In the following Steps, **Lei** will be intro-

duced to more verbs **e Lei** should drill them

in exactly the same way as **Lei** did in this

section. Look up **le parole nuove** in

(dee-tsee-oh-nah-ree-oh)
your **dizionario** **e** make up your own
dictionary

sentences. Try out your **parole nuove** for

that's how you make them yours to use on

your holiday. Remember, the more **Lei**

practice **adesso,** the more enjoyable your trip

(bwoh-nah) (for-too-nah)
will be. **Buona fortuna!**
good luck

LE RISPOSTE

3. Lei ha bisogno di cinquecento euro.
2. Noi impariamo l'italiano.
1. Io parlo italiano.

6. Lei compra un libro.
5. Loro abitano in Canada.
4. Lui viene dall'albergo.

45

(keh) *(oh-reh)* *(soh-noh)*
Che ore sono?
what   time   is it

Lei know how to tell **i** *(jor-nee)* **giorni della settimana e i mesi dell' anno,** so now let's learn to tell
           days   week   months   year

time. As a traveler **in Italia, Lei** need to be able to tell time in order to make **prenotazioni**
                                             (preh-noh-tah-tsee-oh-nee)
                                             reservations

(ahp-poon-tah-men-tee) *(treh-nee)*
e appuntamenti, e to catch **treni e autobus. Ecco** the "basics."
appointments   trains   buses   here are

What time is it?	=	*(keh) (oh-reh)* **Che ore sono?** _____
noon	=	*(med-zoh-jor-noh)* **il mezzogiorno** _____
midnight	=	*(med-zah-noht-teh)* **la mezzanotte** _____
half past	=	*(med-zoh)* **e mezzo** _____
minus	=	*(meh-noh)* **meno** _____
a quarter	=	*(kwar-toh)* **un quarto** _____
a quarter to / before	=	*(meh-noh)* **meno un quarto** _____
a quarter after / past	=	*(eh) (kwar-toh)* **e un quarto** _____

Adesso quiz yourself. Fill in the missing letters below.

midnight = `m` `e` `☐` `☐` `a` `n` `o` `☐` `☐` `e`   minus = `m` `e` `☐` `☐`

quarter before = `m` `e` `n` `☐` `☒` `n` `☒` `☐` `a` `r` `t` `o`

half past = `☐` `☒` `m` `e` `☐` `☐` `o`   and finally

What time is it? `C` `h` `☐` `☒` `o` `r` `☐` `☒` `☐` `☐` `☐` `?`

❏ **il Papa** *(pah-pah)*	Pope	_____
❏ **il parcheggio** *(par-keh-joh)*	parking place/lot	_____
❏ **il parco** *(par-koh)*	park	_____
❏ **Parigi** *(pah-ree-jee)*	Paris	**p**
❏ **la parte** *(par-teh)*	part, portion	_____

Adesso, come are these **parole** used? Study **gli esempi** below. When **Lei** think it through, it
(how) _(l-yee) (eh-zem-pee)_
(examples)

really is not too difficult. Just notice that the pattern changes after the halfway mark. Notice

that the phrase "o'clock" is not used in Italian.

Sono le **cinque.** _(cheen-kweh)_
_it is_ _five o'clock_

`5:00`

<u>Sono le cinque. Sono le cinque.</u>

Sono le cinque e **dieci.** _(dee-eh-chee)_

`5:10`

_____

Sono le cinque e **un quarto.** _(kwar-toh)_
and a _quarter_

`5:15`

_____

Sono le cinque e **venti.** _(ven-tee)_

`5:20`

_____

Sono le cinque e **mezzo.** _(med-zoh)_
half past five

`5:30`

_____

Sono le **sei meno venti.** _(seh-ee)(meh-noh)_

`5:40`

_____

Sono le sei meno un quarto.

`5:45`

_____

Sono le sei meno dieci.

`5:50`

_____

Sono le **sei.** _(seh-ee)_

`6:00`

_____

See how **importante** learning **i numeri** is? Answer the following **domande** based on **gli**
(eem-por-tahn-teh) _(noo-meh-ree)_ _(doh-mahn-deh)_ _(l-yee)_
(questions)

orologi below. _(oh-roh-loh-jee)_
clocks

1. `8:00` _____

2. `7:15` _____

3. `4:30` _____

4. `9:20` _____

LE RISPOSTE

4. Sono le nove e venti.

3. Sono le quattro e mezzo.

2. Sono le sette e un quarto.

1. Sono le otto.

47

When **Lei** answer a "**quando?**" *(kwahn-doh)* question, say "**alle**" *(ahl-leh)* before **Lei** give the time. Remember **in**
when at

Italia they use the 24-hour clock so 6 p.m. is 18:00!

1. **Quando viene il treno?** _____ *alle sei* _____
   (kwahn-doh) *(vee-eh-neh)* *(treh-noh)*
   comes train (at 6:00)

2. **Quando viene l'autobus?** _____
   (lah-oo-toh-boos)
   comes bus (at 7:30)

3. **Quando comincia il concerto?** _____
   (koh-meen-chah) *(kohn-chair-toh)*
   begins / commences concert (at 21:00)

4. **Quando comincia il film?** _____
   (feelm)
   begins film (at 22:00)

5. **Quando apre il ristorante?** _____
   (ah-preh) *(ree-stoh-rahn-teh)*
   opens (at 11:30)

6. **Quando apre la banca?** _____
   (bahn-kah)
   (at 8:30)

7. **Quando chiude il ristorante?** _____
   (kee-oo-deh)
   closes (at 14:00)

8. **Quando chiude la banca?** _____
   closes (at 17:00)

Ecco a quick quiz. Fill in the blanks **con** the correct **numeri**.
here is with *(kohn)*

9. **Un minuto ha** _____ **secondi.**
   (mee-noo-toh) *(ah)* (?) *(seh-kohn-dee)*
   minute has seconds

10. **Un'ora ha** _____ **minuti.**
   (oo-noh-rah) *(ah)* (?)
   hour has minutes

11. **Una settimana ha** _____ **giorni.**
   (oo-nah) *(ah)* (?) *(jor-nee)*
   week days

12. **Un anno ha** _____ **mesi.**
   (ahn-noh) *(ah)* (?) *(meh-zee)*
   year has months

13. **Un anno ha** _____ **settimane.**
   (?) *(set-tee-mah-neh)*
   weeks

14. **Un anno ha** _____ **giorni.**
   (?) *(jor-nee)*

LE RISPOSTE

1. alle sei
2. alle sette e mezzo
3. alle ventuno
4. alle ventidue
5. alle undici e mezzo
6. alle otto e mezzo
7. alle quattordici
8. alle diciassette

9. sessanta
10. sessanta
11. sette
12. dodici
13. cinquantadue
14. trecentosessantacinque

Do **Lei** remember your greetings from earlier? It is a good time to review them as they will

always be **molto** *(mohl-toh)* **importanti.**
very   important

Alle otto di mattina, *(ah-leh)* *(dee)* **si dice,** *(see)(dee-cheh)* **"Buon giorno, signora Fellini."** *(jor-noh)* *(seen-yoh-rah)*
at   in the morning   one says   good   morning

Che diciamo? *(dee-chah-moh)* _____ *Buon giorno, signora Fellini.* _____
what   do we say

Alle tredici, si dice, "Buon giorno, signor Franchi." *(seen-yor)* *(frahn-kee)*
Mr.

Che diciamo? _____

Alle diciannove, *(dee-chahn-noh-veh)* **si dice, "Buona sera, signorina Moretti."** *(seen-yoh-ree-nah)*
Miss

Che diciamo? *(keh)* _____

Alle ventidue, si dice, "Buona *(see)* **notte,** *(bwoh-nah) (noht-teh)* **Antonio."**
night

Che diciamo? _____

Lei have probably already noticed that plurals are *generally* formed in the following way.

la macchina *(mahk-kee-nah)*   **le macchine** *(mahk-kee-neh)*
bicycle   bicycles

l' ora *(loh-rah)*   **le ore** *(oh-reh)*
hour   hours

il cane *(kah-neh)*   **i cani** *(kah-nee)*
dog   dogs

il gatto *(gaht-toh)*   **i gatti** *(gaht-tee)*
cat   cats

In italiano adjectives agree with the gender and number of the nouns they modify **e** they

generally come after the noun (but not always!)

la macchina rossa *(rohs-sah)*   **le macchine rosse** *(rohs-seh)*
red

il telefono nero *(neh-roh)*   **i telefoni neri** *(neh-ree)*
black

❑	**la partenza** *(par-ten-tsah)*	departure	
❑	**il passaporto** *(pahs-sah-por-toh)*	passport	
❑	**la pasta** *(pah-stah)*	pasta, pastry **p**	
❑	**la patata** *(pah-tah-tah)*	potato	
❑	**la penna** *(pen-nah)*	pen	

Ecco due verbi nuovi per *(pair)* Step 13.
for

(mahn-jah-reh)
mangiare _____
to eat

(beh-reh)
bere _____
to drink

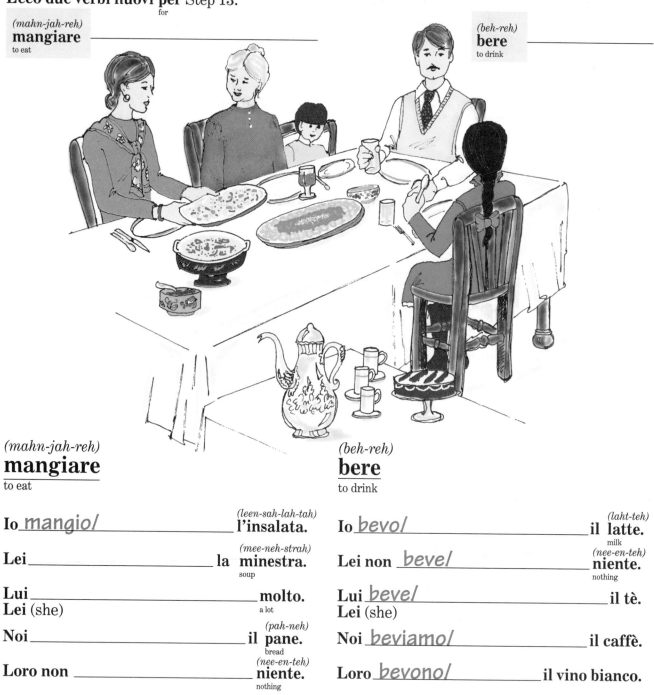

(mahn-jah-reh)
mangiare
to eat

(beh-reh)
bere
to drink

Io <u>mangio/</u> _____ l'insalata.
(leen-sah-lah-tah)

Lei _____ la minestra.
(mee-neh-strah)
soup

Lui _____ molto.
Lei (she)
a lot

Noi _____ il pane.
(pah-neh)
bread

Loro non _____ niente.
(nee-en-teh)
nothing

Io <u>bevo/</u> _____ il latte.
(laht-teh)
milk

Lei non <u>beve/</u> _____ niente.
(nee-en-teh)
nothing

Lui <u>beve/</u> _____ il tè.
Lei (she)

Noi <u>beviamo/</u> _____ il caffè.

Loro <u>bevono/</u> _____ il vino bianco.

Lei have learned that to negate a statement, simply add **<u>non</u>** before the verb. Notice in the

examples above, that when you use the word "**<u>niente</u>**," you also need to add "**<u>non</u>**" before the verb.
nothing

(dee-koh) (nee-en-teh)
Io non dico niente.
I   say   nothing

Noi non compriamo niente.
we   buy   nothing

OR

Non dico niente.

Non compriamo niente.

(leh-ee)
Lei have learned a lot of material in the last few steps **e** that means it is time to quiz yourself. Don't panic, this is just for you **e** no one else needs to know how **Lei** did. Remember, this is a chance to review, find out what **Lei** remember **e** what **Lei** need to spend more time on. After **Lei** have finished, check your **risposte** in the glossary at the back of this book. Circle the correct answers.

il caffè	tea	coffee
no	yes	no
la zia	aunt	uncle
o	and	or
imparare	to drink	to learn
mattina	morning	night
martedì	Friday	Tuesday
parlare	to live	to speak
(leh-stah-teh) l'estate	summer	winter
il denaro	money	page
dieci	nine	ten
molto	a lot	bread

la famiglia	seven	family
i figli	children	grandfather
il latte	butter	(milk)
il sale	pepper	salt
sotto	under	over
il medico	man	doctor
giugno	June	July
la cucina	kitchen	religions
(oh) ho	I need	I have
comprare	to take	to buy
(ee-eh-ree) ieri	yesterday	tomorrow
(jahl-loh) giallo	good	yellow

(koh-meh)
Come sta?   What time is it?   How are you?   Well, how are you after this quiz?

14

(nord) (sood) (est) (oh-vest)
Nord - Sud, Est - Ovest
north   south   east   west

(kar-tah) (jeh-oh-grah-fee-kah)
If **Lei** are looking at **una carta geografica** e **Lei** see the following **parole,** it should not be too

difficult to figure out what they mean. Take an educated guess.

(lah-meh-ree-kah)
l'America del nord

(lah-meh-ree-kah) (sood)
l'America del sud

il Polo nord

il Polo sud

(dah-koh-tah)
il Dakota del nord

(kah-roo-lee-nah)
la Carolina del sud

(leer-lahn-dah)
l'Irlanda del nord

(sood-ah-free-kah)
il Sudafrica

(pair)
Le parole italiane per "north," "south," "east" e "west" are easy to recognize due to their

similitudini to **inglese.** These **parole sono molto importanti.** Learn them **oggi!**
are   (oh-jee)

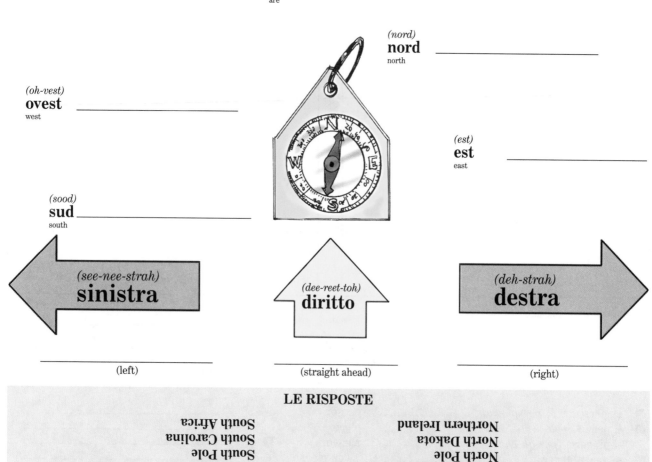

(nord)
nord _____
north

(oh-vest)
ovest _____
west

(est)
est _____
east

(sood)
sud _____
south

(see-nee-strah)
sinistra

(dee-reet-toh)
diritto

(deh-strah)
destra

_____ (left)

_____ (straight ahead)

_____ (right)

These **parole** can go a long way. Say them aloud each time you write them in the blanks below.

(pair) (fah-voh-reh)
per favore _____
please

(grah-tsee-eh)
grazie _____
thank you

(mee) (skoo-zee)
mi scusi _____
excuse me

(preh-goh)
prego _____
you're welcome

(kohn-vair-sah-tsee-oh-nee)   (tee-pee-keh) (pair)
Ecco due conversazioni   very **tipiche per** someone who is trying to find something.
two   conversations   typical   for

Write them out in the blanks below.

(lahl-bair-goh)
Gianni: **Mi scusi. Dov'è l'Albergo Florio?**
              excuse me

_____ **Mi scusi. Dov'è l'Albergo Florio?** _____

(kohn-tee-noo-ee) (dee-reet-toh) (poy) (jee-ree)   (een-kroh-choh)
Pietro: **Continui   diritto,   poi giri   a sinistra al secondo incrocio.**
              straight ahead then turn   crossing

_____

(lee)
L'Albergo Florio è lì   a destra.
              there to the right

_____

(veel-lah) (joo-lee-ah)
Stefano: **Mi scusi. Dov'è la Villa Giulia?**

_____

(jee-ree) (kwee)   (kohn-tee-noo-ee)   (pair) (chen-toh) (meh-tree)
Andrea: **Giri   qui a destra. Continui   diritto per cento metri.**
              turn   here   meters

_____

(poy)   (ahl-lahn-goh-loh)
Poi giri a sinistra e la Villa Giulia è all'angolo.
then   at the corner

_____

❏	**il piatto** (pee-aht-toh)	plate, dish	_____
❏	**la piazza** (pee-ah-tsah)	plaza, town square	_____
❏	**la pillola** (peel-loh-lah)	pill	_____
❏	**pittoresco** (peet-toh-reh-skoh)	picturesque	_____
❏	**la polizia** (poh-lee-tsee-ah)	police	_____

p

53

Are **Lei** lost? There is no need to be lost if **Lei ha** *(ah)* / have learned the basic **parole di direzione.** *(dee-reh-tsee-oh-neh)* / direction

Do not try to memorize these **conversazioni** because **Lei** will never be looking for precisely these places. One day, **Lei** might need to ask **direzioni** / directions to "**il Foro Romano**" *(foh-roh) (roh-mah-noh)* / Roman Forum or "**il Colosseo.**" *(koh-lohs-seh-oh)* / Colosseum

Learn the key direction **parole e** be sure **Lei** can find your **destinazione.** *(deh-stee-nah-tsee-oh-neh)* / destination **Lei** may want to buy a guidebook to start planning which places **Lei** would like to visit. Practice asking **direzioni** to these special places. What if the person responding to your **domanda** / question answers too quickly for **Lei** to understand the entire reply? Practice saying,

Mi scusi. Io non capisco. Ripeta, per favore!
I / do not / understand *(kah-pee-skoh)* / *(ree-peh-tah)* repeat / *(pair)*

Adesso, say it again **e** then write it out below.

_____

(Excuse me. I do not understand. Please repeat.)

Sì, *(see)* / yes **è difficile** / difficult at first but don't give up! **Quando** / when the directions are repeated, **Lei** will be able to understand if **Lei ha** *(ah)* / have learned the key **parole.** Let's review by writing them in the blanks below.

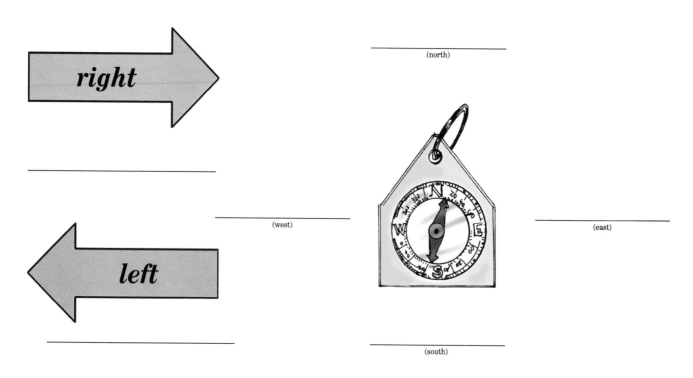

right

left

_____ (north)

_____ (west)

_____ (east)

_____ (south)

☐ **la porta** *(por-tah)* .... door
☐ **il porto** *(por-toh)* .... port
☐ **la porzione** *(por-tsee-oh-neh)* .... portion   **p**
☐ **possibile** *(pohs-see-bee-leh)* .... possible
☐ **la posta** *(poh-stah)* .... post office, mail

_____
_____
_____
_____
_____

54

Ecco quattro verbi nuovi. *(noo-oh-vee)*
verbs   new

(troh-vah-reh)
trovare _____
to find

(kah-pee-reh)
capire _____
to understand

(ven-deh-reh)
vendere _____
to sell

(ree-peh-teh-reh)
ripetere _____
to repeat

As always, say each sentence out loud. Say each **e** every **parola** carefully, pronouncing each

Italian sound as well as **Lei** can.

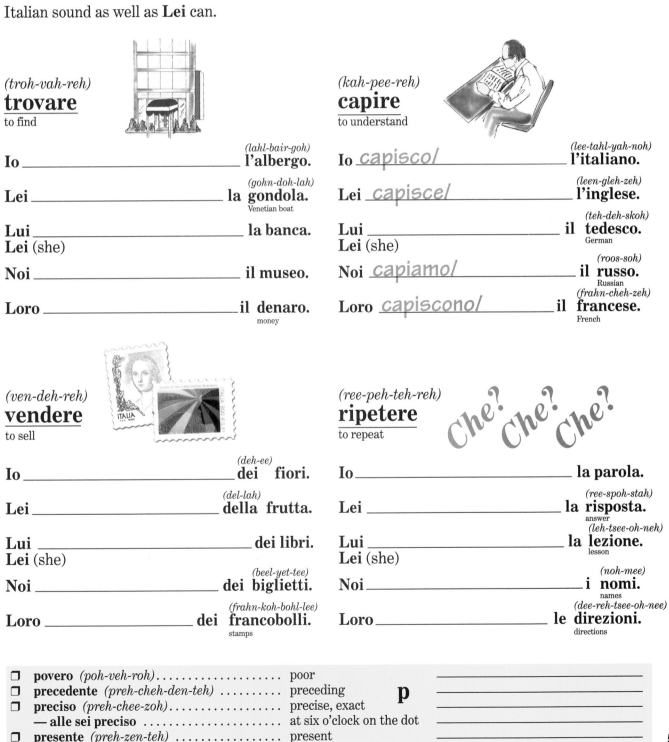

(troh-vah-reh)
trovare
to find

Io _____ l'albergo. *(lahl-bair-goh)*

Lei _____ la gondola. *(gohn-doh-lah)*
Venetian boat

Lui _____ la banca.
Lei (she)

Noi _____ il museo.

Loro _____ il denaro.
money

(kah-pee-reh)
capire
to understand

Io _capisco/_ l'italiano. *(lee-tahl-yah-noh)*

Lei _capisce/_ l'inglese. *(leen-gleh-zeh)*

Lui _____ il tedesco. *(teh-deh-skoh)*
Lei (she)   German

Noi _capiamo/_ il russo. *(roos-soh)*
Russian

Loro _capiscono/_ il francese. *(frahn-cheh-zeh)*
French

(ven-deh-reh)
vendere
to sell

Io _____ dei fiori. *(deh-ee)*

Lei _____ della frutta. *(del-lah)*

Lui _____ dei libri.
Lei (she)

Noi _____ dei biglietti. *(beel-yet-tee)*

Loro _____ dei francobolli. *(frahn-koh-bohl-lee)*
stamps

(ree-peh-teh-reh)
ripetere
to repeat

Che? Che? Che?

Io _____ la parola.

Lei _____ la risposta. *(ree-spoh-stah)*
answer

Lui _____ la lezione. *(leh-tsee-oh-neh)*
Lei (she)   lesson

Noi _____ i nomi. *(noh-mee)*
names

Loro _____ le direzioni. *(dee-reh-tsee-oh-nee)*
directions

☐ **povero** *(poh-veh-roh)* . . . . poor
☐ **precedente** *(preh-cheh-den-teh)* . . . . preceding
☐ **preciso** *(preh-chee-zoh)* . . . . precise, exact
    — alle sei preciso . . . . at six o'clock on the dot
☐ **presente** *(preh-zen-teh)* . . . . present

p _____
_____
_____
_____
_____

55

(dee) *(soh-prah)*   *(dee)* *(soht-toh)*

Di Sopra – Di Sotto
above / upstairs   below / downstairs

(ahn-koh-rah)   *(kah-meh-rah)*

Adesso impariamo ancora delle parole. Ecco una casa in Italia. Go to your **camera da**
(we) learn   more   bedroom

letto e look around. Let's learn **i nomi delle cose nella camera** just like we learned the
                                        of the   things   in the

various parts of **la casa.**

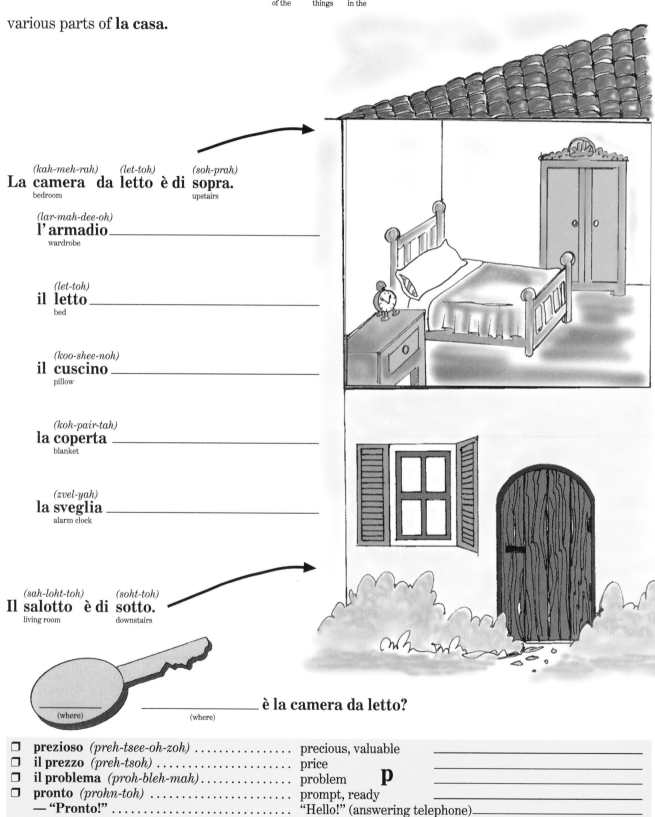

(kah-meh-rah)   *(let-toh)*   *(soh-prah)*

La camera da letto è di sopra.
bedroom   upstairs

(lar-mah-dee-oh)
l'armadio _____
wardrobe

(let-toh)
il letto _____
bed

(koo-shee-noh)
il cuscino _____
pillow

(koh-pair-tah)
la coperta _____
blanket

(zvel-yah)
la sveglia _____
alarm clock

(sah-loht-toh)   *(soht-toh)*

Il salotto è di sotto.
living room   downstairs

_____ _____ **è la camera da letto?**
(where)   (where)

☐ **prezioso** *(preh-tsee-oh-zoh)*	precious, valuable	_____
☐ **il prezzo** *(preh-tsoh)*	price	_____
☐ **il problema** *(proh-bleh-mah)*	problem **p**	_____
☐ **pronto** *(prohn-toh)*	prompt, ready	_____
— **"Pronto!"**	"Hello!" (answering telephone)	_____

Adesso, remove the next **quattro** stickers **e** label these **cose nella Sua** *(soo-ah)* **camera da letto.** Let's
_{your}

move into **il bagno** *(bahn-yoh)* **e** do the same thing. Remember, **il bagno** means a room to bathe in. If **Lei**
_{bathroom}

è in un ristorante e Lei ha *(ah)* **bisogno** *(bee-zohn-yoh)* **del** lavatory, **Lei** want to ask for **i gabinetti** *(gah-bee-net-tee)* **e** *not* for
_{need}

il bagno. Restrooms may be marked with pictures **o** simply **"signore" e "signori."**
_{or}

Don't confuse them!

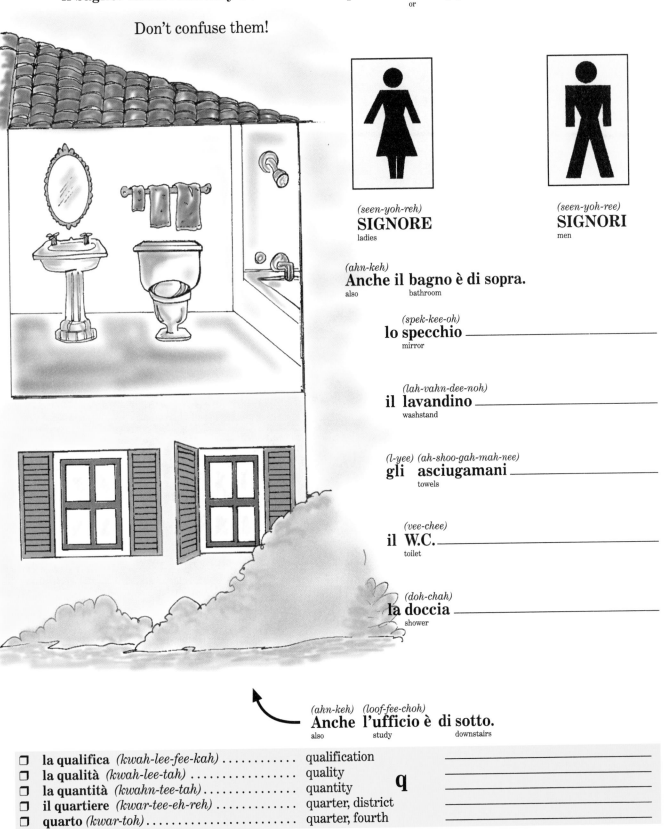

(seen-yoh-reh)
SIGNORE
ladies

(seen-yoh-ree)
SIGNORI
men

(ahn-keh)
Anche il bagno è di sopra.
also   bathroom

(spek-kee-oh)
lo specchio _____
mirror

(lah-vahn-dee-noh)
il lavandino _____
washstand

(l-yee) (ah-shoo-gah-mah-nee)
gli asciugamani _____
towels

(vee-chee)
il W.C. _____
toilet

(doh-chah)
la doccia _____
shower

(ahn-keh) (loof-fee-choh)
Anche l'ufficio è di sotto.
also   study   downstairs

❐ **la qualifica** *(kwah-lee-fee-kah)*	qualification	_____
❐ **la qualità** *(kwah-lee-tah)*	quality	_____
❐ **la quantità** *(kwahn-tee-tah)*	quantity **q**	_____
❐ **il quartiere** *(kwar-tee-eh-reh)*	quarter, district	_____
❐ **quarto** *(kwar-toh)*	quarter, fourth	_____

Non forget to remove the next group of stickers **e** label these things in your **bagno.** Okay, it is time to review. Here's a quick quiz to see what you remember.

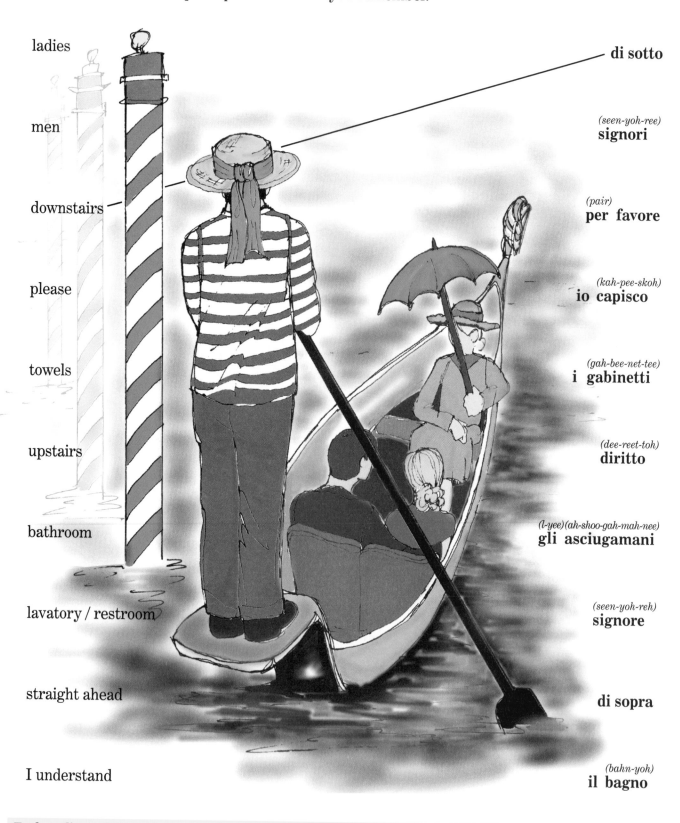

ladies

men

downstairs

please

towels

upstairs

bathroom

lavatory / restroom

straight ahead

I understand

di sotto

(seen-yoh-ree)
signori

(pair)
per favore

(kah-pee-skoh)
io capisco

(gah-bee-net-tee)
i gabinetti

(dee-reet-toh)
diritto

(l-yee)(ah-shoo-gah-mah-nee)
gli asciugamani

(seen-yoh-reh)
signore

di sopra

(bahn-yoh)
il bagno

❐	**la radio** *(rah-dee-oh)*	. . . .	radio	
❐	**la ragione** *(rah-joh-neh)*	. . . .	reason	
❐	**rapido** *(rah-pee-doh)*	. . . .	rapid, fast	**r**
❐	**recente** *(reh-chen-teh)*	. . . .	recent	
❐	**il resto** *(reh-stoh)*	. . . .	rest, change (money)	

Next stop — **l'ufficio,** *(loof-fee-choh)* office specifically **il tavolo** *(tah-voh-loh)* table **o la scrivania** *(skree-vah-nee-ah)* desk **nell'ufficio.** *(nel-loof-fee-choh)* **Che** *(keh)* **c'è** *(cheh)* is there **sulla** *(sool-lah)* on the

scrivania? Let's identify **le cose** things which one normally finds **sulla scrivania** or strewn about

(loof-fee-choh)
l'ufficio.

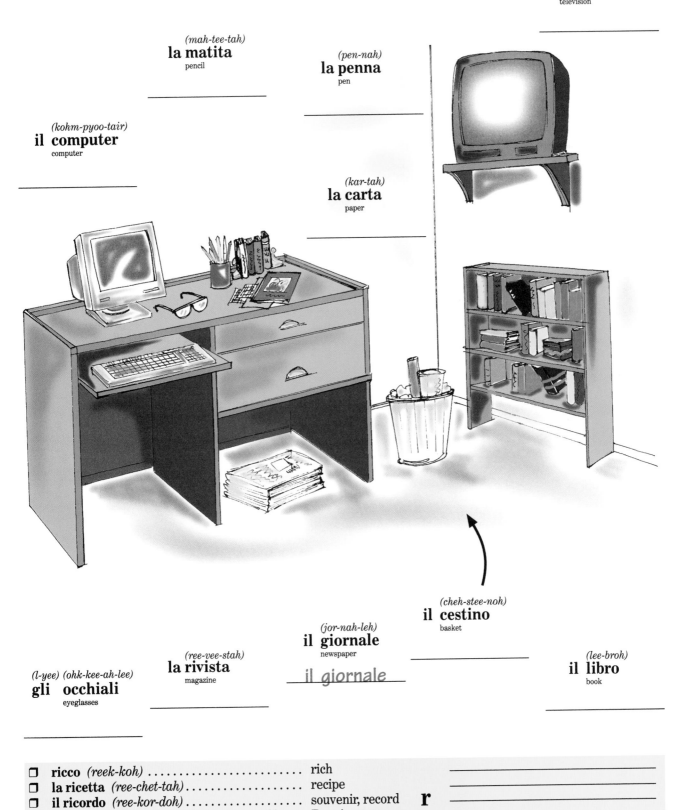

(teh-leh-vee-zee-oh-neh)
la televisione
television

(mah-tee-tah)
la matita
pencil

(pen-nah)
la penna
pen

(kohm-pyoo-tair)
il computer
computer

(kar-tah)
la carta
paper

(cheh-stee-noh)
il cestino
basket

(jor-nah-leh)
il giornale
newspaper

il giornale

(ree-vee-stah)
la rivista
magazine

(lee-broh)
il libro
book

(l-yee) (ohk-kee-ah-lee)
gli occhiali
eyeglasses

☐ **ricco** *(reek-koh)*	rich		
☐ **la ricetta** *(ree-chet-tah)*	recipe		
☐ **il ricordo** *(ree-kor-doh)*	souvenir, record	**r**	
☐ **il Rinascimento** *(ree-nah-shee-men-toh)*	Renaissance		
☐ **il rispetto** *(ree-spet-toh)*	respect		

Don't forget these essentials!

(let-teh-rah)
la lettera
letter

(frahn-koh-bohl-loh)
il **francobollo**
stamp

(kar-toh-lee-nah)
la cartolina
postcard

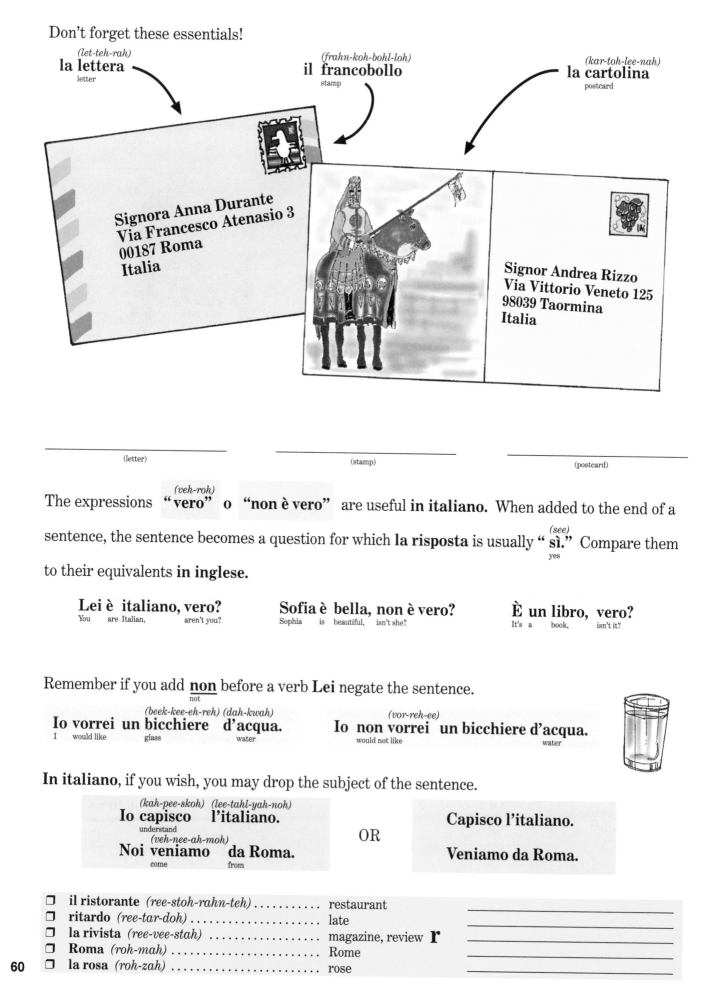

Signora Anna Durante
Via Francesco Atenasio 3
00187 Roma
Italia

Signor Andrea Rizzo
Via Vittorio Veneto 125
98039 Taormina
Italia

_____ (letter) _____ (stamp) _____ (postcard)

The expressions *(veh-roh)* **"vero"** o **"non è vero"** are useful **in italiano.** When added to the end of a sentence, the sentence becomes a question for which **la risposta** is usually " *(see)* **sì.**" Compare them
yes
to their equivalents **in inglese.**

Lei è italiano, vero?
You are Italian, aren't you?

Sofia è bella, non è vero?
Sophia is beautiful, isn't she?

È un libro, vero?
It's a book, isn't it?

Remember if you add **non** before a verb **Lei** negate the sentence.
not

(beek-kee-eh-reh) (dah-kwah)
Io vorrei un bicchiere d'acqua.
I would like glass water

(vor-reh-ee)
Io non vorrei un bicchiere d'acqua.
would not like water

In italiano, if you wish, you may drop the subject of the sentence.

(kah-pee-skoh) (lee-tahl-yah-noh)
Io capisco l'italiano.
understand
(veh-nee-ah-moh)
Noi veniamo da Roma.
come from

OR

Capisco l'italiano.

Veniamo da Roma.

☐ **il ristorante** *(ree-stoh-rahn-teh)* . . . . restaurant
☐ **ritardo** *(ree-tar-doh)* . . . . late
☐ **la rivista** *(ree-vee-stah)* . . . . magazine, review **r**
☐ **Roma** *(roh-mah)* . . . . Rome
☐ **la rosa** *(roh-zah)* . . . . rose

Simple, isn't it? **Adesso**, after you fill in the blanks below, go back a second time and negate all these sentences by adding **"non"** before each verb. Then go back a third time **e** drop the subject. Don't get discouraged! Just look at how much **Lei** have already learned **e** think ahead to

(tor-reh) *(pen-den-teh)*
pasta, la Torre Pendente e new adventures.
Leaning Tower

(veh-deh-reh)
vedere _____
to see

(dor-mee-reh)
dormire _____
to sleep

(mahn-dah-reh)
mandare _____
to send

(fah-reh)
fare _____
to do, to make

(veh-deh-reh)
vedere
to see

Io _____ il **mercato.** *(mair-kah-toh)*

Lei _vede/_ il **Museo Borghese.**

Lui _____ il **Colosseo.** *(koh-lohs-seh-oh)*
Lei (she)   Colosseum

Noi _____ il **Mare Mediterraneo.**
                     Mediterranean Sea

Loro _____ le **montagne.** *(mohn-tahn-yeh)*
                                              mountains

(mahn-dah-reh)
mandare
to send

Io _____ la **lettera.** *(let-teh-rah)*
                                            letter

Lei _____ la **cartolina.**

Lui _manda/_ il **libro.**
Lei (she)

Noi _____ due **cartoline.** *(kar-toh-lee-neh)*
                                                postcards

Loro _____ tre **lettere.**

(dor-mee-reh)
dormire
to sleep

Io_____ nella **camera.** *(kah-meh-rah)*

Lei _____ in un **albergo.**

Lui _dorme/_ a **casa.**
Lei (she)

Noi _____ sotto la **coperta.** *(koh-pair-tah)*
                             under   blanket

Loro _____ **senza** i **cuscini.** *(sen-zah)* *(koo-shee-nee)*
                              without   pillows

(fah-reh)
fare
to do, to make

Io _faccio/_ **tutto.** *(toot-toh)*
                        everything

Lei _fa/_ una **telefonata.** *(teh-leh-foh-nah-tah)*
                              telephone call

Lui _____ **molto.** *(mohl-toh)*
Lei (she)   a lot

Noi non _facciamo/_ **niente.** *(nee-en-teh)*
                                nothing

Loro _fanno/_ **tutto.** *(toot-toh)*
                         everything

❐ **il sacco** *(sahk-koh)*.....................	sack, bag	
❐ **il sale** *(sah-leh)*.........................	salt	**S** _____
— **Sali e Tabacchi**	salt and tobacco store	_____
❐ **la salsa** *(sahl-sah)*	sauce	_____
❐ **il saluto** *(sah-loo-toh)*	greeting, salutation	_____

61

Before **Lei** proceed with the next step, **per favore** identify all the items *(kwee)* **qui sotto.**
here

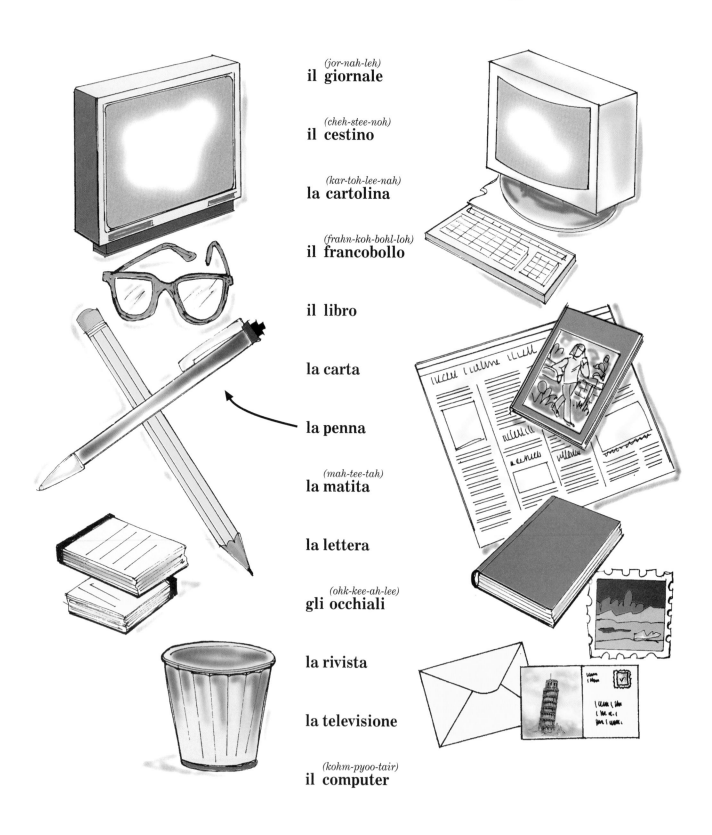

(jor-nah-leh)
il giornale

(cheh-stee-noh)
il cestino

(kar-toh-lee-nah)
la cartolina

(frahn-koh-bohl-loh)
il francobollo

il libro

la carta

la penna

(mah-tee-tah)
la matita

la lettera

(ohk-kee-ah-lee)
gli occhiali

la rivista

la televisione

(kohm-pyoo-tair)
il computer

❏	**la scala** *(skah-lah)*	staircase, stairs	
	— la Scala	opera house in Milan	
❏	**lo scavo** *(skah-voh)*	excavation	**S**
❏	**la scena** *(sheh-nah)*	scene	
❏	**la scienza** *(shee-en-zah)*	science	

Adesso **Lei** *(leh-ee)* know how to count, how to ask **domande**, how to use **verbi con** the "plug-in" questions

formula **e** how to describe something, be it the location of **un albergo o il colore d'una casa**. house

Let's take the basics that **Lei ha** learned **e** expand them in special areas that will be most helpful

in your travels. What does everyone do on a holiday? Send postcards, **non è vero?** *(veh-roh)* Let's don't they

learn exactly how **l'ufficio postale** *(poh-stah-leh)* **italiano** works. post office

la posta *(poh-stah)* mail

in Spagna *(spahn-yah)* to

in Inghilterra *(een-gheel-tair-rah)*

in Francia *(frahn-chah)*

in America *(ah-meh-ree-kah)*

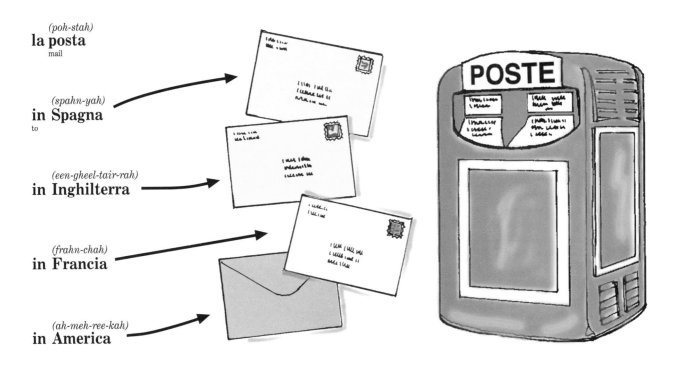

The **PT** *(pee-tee)* **(Poste e Telecomunicazioni)** *(teh-leh-koh-moo-nee-kah-tsee-oh-nee)* is where **Lei** buy **francobolli**, send **pacchi**, post office   packages

cartoline e lettere. Lei may also buy **francobolli** at the local **tabaccheria** *(tah-bahk-keh-ree-ah)* of which there are tobacco shop

many. If **Lei ha bisogno** *(bee-zohn-yoh)* to call home **in America,** this can also be done at the **PT. Le PT** *(pee-tee)*

sono closed on Sunday.

❏ **secondo** *(seh-kohn-doh)*	second	_____
❏ **il segnale** *(sen-yah-leh)*	signal, sign	_____
❏ **il segretario** *(seh-greh-tah-ree-oh)*	secretary (male) **S**	_____
❏ **la selezione** *(seh-leh-tsee-oh-neh)*	selection, choice	_____
❏ **la semisfera** *(seh-mee-sfeh-rah)*	hemisphere	_____

Ecco some **parole necessarie** *(neh-ches-sah-ree-eh)* **per l'ufficio postale.** Practice them aloud **e** then write them in the blanks.

(let-teh-rah)
la lettera
letter

(kar-toh-lee-nah)
la cartolina
postcard

_____

_____

(pahk-koh)
il pacco
package

(lee-mail)
l'email
email

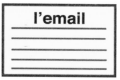

_____

_____

(vee-ah) (ah-eh-reh-ah)
via aerea
by airmail

(fahx)
il fax

_____

_____

(frahn-koh-bohl-loh)
il francobollo
stamp

(kah-bee-nah)(teh-leh-foh-nee-kah)
la cabina telefonica
telephone booth

_____

_____

(boo-kah) (del-leh) (let-teh-reh)
la buca delle lettere
mailbox

(teh-leh-foh-noh)
il telefono

_____

_____

❏ **semplice** *(sem-plee-cheh)*	simple, easy	
❏ **il sentimento** *(sen-tee-men-toh)*	feeling	
❏ **serio** *(seh-ree-oh)*	serious	**s**
❏ **il servizio** *(sair-vee-tsee-oh)*	service	
❏ **sfortunato** *(sfor-too-nah-toh)*	unfortunate, unlucky	

_____

_____

_____

_____

_____

64

Next step — **Lei** ask **domande** like those **sotto,** depending on what **Lei vorrebbe.** Repeat

questions   *(vor-reb-beh)*
                                               would like

these sentences aloud many times.

Dove compro dei francobolli?_____
do I buy

Dove compro una cartolina?_____

(fah-choh)   *(teh-leh-foh-nah-tah)* *(een-tair-oor-bah-nah)*
Dove faccio una telefonata   interurbana?_____
do I make   *telephone call*   *long-distance*

(boo-kah)   *(let-teh-reh)*
Dov'è una buca delle lettere?_____
where is   *mailbox*

                  (teh-leh-foh-nee-kah)
Dov'è una cabina telefonica?_____
telephone booth

(mahn-doh)   *(pahk-koh)*
Dove mando un pacco?_____
do I send

(fah-choh)
Dove faccio una telefonata?_____
do I make   *telephone call*

Quanto costa?_____*Quanto costa? Quanto costa?*_____
how much

Adesso, quiz yourself. See if **Lei** can translate the following thoughts **in italiano.**

1.   Where is a telephone booth?_____

2.   Where do I make a telephone call? _____

3.   Where do I make a long-distance telephone call? _____

4.   Where is the post office? _____

5.   Where do I buy stamps? _____

6.   Airmail stamps? _____

7.   Where do I send a package? _____

8.   Where do I send a fax? _____

65

Ecco quattro verbi nuovi.
verbs

(ah-spet-tah-reh)
aspettare _____
to wait (for)

(mee) (dee-ah)
mi dia . . . _____
give me

(skree-veh-reh)
scrivere _____
to write

(pah-gah-reh)
pagare _____
to pay (for)

Practice these verbs by not only filling in the blanks, but by saying them aloud many, many times until you are comfortable with the sounds **e** the words.

(ah-spet-tah-reh)
aspettare
to wait (for)

Io _aspetto/_ il **treno.** *(treh-noh)*

Lei _____ **l'autobus.** *(lah-oo-toh-boos)*

Lui _____ **il tassì.** *(tahs-see)*
Lei (she) taxi

Noi _____ in **albergo.** *(ahl-bair-goh)*
hotel

Loro _____ davanti all'**albergo.**

(skree-veh-reh)
scrivere
to write

Io _____ **l'indirizzo.** *(leen-dee-ree-tsoh)*
address

Lei _scrive/_ **molto.** *(nee-en-teh)*
a lot

Lui non _____ **niente.** *(nee-en-teh)*
Lei (she) nothing

Noi _____ **due lettere.** *(doo-eh)*

Loro _____ **i loro nomi.**
their names

(mee) (dee-ah)
mi dia . . .
give me

Mi dia/ il **conto, per favore.** *(kohn-toh) (pair)*
bill

_____ il **menù, per favore.** *(meh-noo)*

_____ il **biglietto, per favore.** *(beel-yet-toh)*

_____ l'**indirizzo, per favore.** *(leen-dee-ree-tsoh)*
address

_____ il **nome, per favore.** *(noh-meh)*
name

(pah-gah-reh)
pagare
to pay (for)

Io _pago/_ il **conto.** *(kohn-toh)*
bill

Lei _paga/_ il **biglietto.** *(beel-yet-toh)*
ticket

Lui _____ la **cena.** *(cheh-nah)*
Lei (she) dinner

Noi _paghiamo/_ **tutto.** *(toot-toh)*
everything

Loro non _pagano/_ **niente.**
nothing

Some of these signs you probably recognize, but take a couple of minutes to review them anyway.

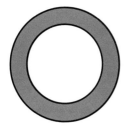

(proh-ee-bee-toh) (lah-ches-soh)
proibito   l'accesso
road closed to vehicles

(doh-gah-nah)
dogana
customs

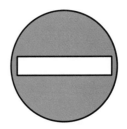

(vee-eh-tah-toh) (lah-ches-soh)
vietato   l'accesso
no entrance

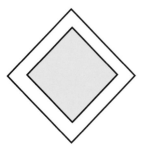

(strah-dah)
strada principale
main road, you have the right of way

(cheh-deh-reh) (eel) (pahs-soh)
cedere   il   passo
yield

(lee-mee-teh) (dee) (veh-loh-chee-tah)
limite   di velocità
speed limit

(dee-vee-eh-toh)   (soh-stah)
divieto   di sosta
no parking

(dee-vee-eh-toh)   (sor-pahs-soh)
divieto   di sorpasso
no passing

(ahlt)
alt
stop

(deh-vee-ah-tsee-oh-neh)
DEVIAZIONE
detour

What follows are approximate conversions, so when you order something by liters, kilograms or grams you will have an idea of what to expect and not find yourself being handed one piece of candy when you thought you ordered an entire bag.

To Convert		Do the Math		
liters (l) to gallons,	multiply by 0.26	4 liters x 0.26	=	1.04 gallons
gallons to liters,	multiply by 3.79	10 gal. x 3.79	=	37.9 liters
kilograms (kg) to pounds,	multiply by 2.2	2 kilograms x 2.2	=	4.4 pounds
pounds to kilos,	multiply by 0.46	10 pounds x 0.46	=	4.6 kg
grams (g) to ounces,	multiply by 0.035	100 grams x 0.035	=	3.5 oz.
ounces to grams,	multiply by 28.35	10 oz. x 28.35	=	283.5 g.
meters (m) to feet,	multiply by 3.28	2 meters x 3.28	=	6.56 feet
feet to meters,	multiply by 0.3	6 feet x 0.3	=	1.8 meters

For fun, take your weight in pounds and convert it into kilograms. It sounds better that way, doesn't it? How many kilometers is it from your home to school, to work, to the post office?

The Simple Versions		
one liter	=	approximately one US quart
four liters	=	approximately one US gallon
one kilo	=	approximately 2.2 pounds
100 grams	=	approximately 3.5 ounces
500 grams	=	slightly more than one pound
one meter	=	slightly more than three feet

The distance between **New York e Roma è** approximately 4,278 miles. How many kilometers would that be? It is only 907 miles between **London e Roma**. How many kilometers is that?

kilometers (km.) to miles,	multiply by 0.62	1000 km. x 0.62	=	620 miles
miles to kilometers,	multiply by 1.6	1000 miles x 1.6	=	1,600 km.

Inches	1	2	3	4	5	6	7

To convert centimeters into inches, multiply by 0.39   Example: 9 cm. x 0.39 = 3.51 in.

To convert inches into centimeters, multiply by 2.54   Example: 4 in. x 2.54 = 10.16 cm.

cm 1	2	3	4	5	6	7	8	9	10	11	12	13	14	15	16	17	18

(chee)

Sì, ci sono anche bills to pay **in Italia. Lei** have just finished your delicious dinner **e Lei**
there are   also

(vor-reb-beh)   *(fah)*   *(kah-meh-ree-eh-reh)*   *(kah-meh-ree-eh-rah)*   *(kah-meh-ree-eh-reh)*

vorrebbe pagare. Che fa? Lei call for **il cameriere** **o la cameriera. Il cameriere**
would like   do you do   waiter   waitress   waiter

will normally reel off what **Lei ha** eaten while writing rapidly. **Lui** will then place a piece **di**
he

carta sulla tavola, "Fa venti euro." Lei will pay **il cameriere o** perhaps **Lei** will pay **alla cassa.**
it makes (comes to)   cashier's desk

Being a seasoned traveler, **Lei** know that tipping **in Italia** is the same as tipping in America. If

(sair-vee-tsee-oh)

il servizio is not included on **il conto,** leave what you consider an appropriate amount for your
service

(soo-oh) (vee-ah-joh)

cameriere sulla tavola. When **Lei** dine out on **Suo viaggio,** it is always a good idea to make
your   trip

a reservation. It can be difficult to get into a popular **ristorante.** Nevertheless, the experience

is well worth the trouble **Lei** might encounter to obtain a reservation. **E** remember, **Lei** know

enough **italiano** to make a reservation. Just speak slowly and clearly.

❏ **sincero** *(seen-cheh-roh)*	sincere	
❏ **la sinfonia** *(seen-foh-nee-ah)*	symphony	
❏ **il soggetto** *(soh-jet-toh)*	subject **S**	
❏ **solo** *(soh-loh)*	alone, solitary	
❏ **la somma** *(sohm-mah)*	total, sum	

Remember these key **parole** when dining out **all'italiana.** *(ahl-lee-tahl-yah-nah)*
in the Italian manner

(kah-meh-ree-eh-reh)
il cameriere _____
waiter

(kah-meh-ree-eh-rah)
la cameriera _____
waitress

(kohn-toh)
il conto *il conto, il conto, il conto*
bill

(mahn-chah)
la mancia _____
tip

(meh-noo) *(lee-stah)*
il menù / la lista _____
menu

(preh-goh)
prego _____
you're welcome

(mee) (skoo-zee)
mi scusi _____
excuse me

(grah-tsee-eh)
grazie _____
thank you

(pair) (fah-voh-reh) *(pee-ah-cheh-reh)*
per favore / per piacere _____
please

(mee) (dee-ah)
mi dia _____
give me

Ecco una sample **conversazione** involving paying **il conto.**

Gianni:	**Mi scusi. Vorrei pagare il conto, per favore.** to pay *Mi scusi. Vorrei pagare il conto, per favore.*
(lahl-bair-gah-toh-reh) **L' albergatore:** hotelkeeper	*(keh)* **Che camera, per favore?** what room _____
Gianni:	**Camera trecentodieci.** _____
L'albergatore:	**Grazie. Un momento, per piacere.** _____
L'albergatore:	**Ecco il conto.** _____

If **Lei ha** any **problema con i numeri** just ask someone to write out **la cifra** *(cheef-rah)* so that **Lei** can
figure / number
be sure you understand everything correctly, **"Per favore, mi scriva la cifra."** *(mee) (skree-vah)*
for me write

Practice: _____
(Please write the figure for me.)

❏ **la sorpresa** *(sor-preh-zah)* . . . . surprise
❏ **lo spagnolo** *(spahn-yoh-loh)* . . . . Spanish, Spaniard
❏ **lo spettacolo** *(spet-tah-koh-loh)* . . . . spectacle, show **S**
❏ **gli Stati Uniti** *(stah-tee)(oo-nee-tee)* . . . . United States
❏ **lo straniero** *(strah-nee-eh-roh)* . . . . foreigner

70

Adesso, let's take a break from **i conti e il denaro e** learn some **nuove** fun **parole. Lei** can
_{money}_{new}

always practice these **parole** by using your flash cards at the back of this **libro.** Carry these

flash cards in your purse, pocket, briefcase **o** knapsack **e** *use them!*

(ah-pair-toh)
aperto
open

(kee-oo-zoh)
chiuso
closed

(grahn-deh)
grande
big

(peek-koh-loh)
piccolo
small

(sah-loo-teh)
in buona salute
health

(mah-lah-toh)
malato
sick

(bwoh-noh)
buono
good

(kaht-tee-voh)
cattivo
bad

(kahl-doh)
caldo
hot / warm

(fred-doh)
freddo
cold

☐	**straordinario** *(strah-or-dee-nah-ree-oh)*	extraordinary	
☐	**lo studio** *(stoo-dee-oh)*	study, studio	
☐	**il successo** *(soo-ches-soh)*	success	**S**
☐	**sud** *(sood)*	south	
☐	**superiore** *(soo-peh-ree-oh-reh)*	superior, above	

(kor-toh)
corto _____
short

(loon-goh)
lungo _____
long

(len-toh)
lento _____
slow

(veh-loh-cheh) (rah-pee-doh)
veloce / rapido _____
fast

(ahl-toh)
alto _____
tall

(bahs-soh)
basso _____
short

(vek-kee-oh)
vecchio _____
old

(joh-vah-neh)
giovane _____
young

(kah-roh)
caro _____
expensive

(eh-koh-noh-mee-koh)
economico / poco caro _____
inexpensive

(reek-koh)
ricco _____
rich

(poh-veh-roh)
povero _____
poor

(mohl-toh)
molto _____
a lot

(poh-koh)
poco _____
a little

❏ **il tabacco** *(tah-bahk-koh)*	tobacco	
❏ **il tassì** *(tahs-see)*	taxi	
❏ **il tavolo** *(tah-voh-loh)*	table	**t**
— **la tavola calda**	cafeteria	
❏ **il teatro** *(teh-ah-troh)*	theater	

Ecco dei *(deh-ee)* verbi nuovi.
some

(sah-peh-reh)
sapere _____
to know (fact)

(leh-jeh-reh)
leggere _____
to read

(poh-teh-reh)
potere _____
to be able to, can

(doh-veh-reh)
dovere _____
to have to, must, to owe

Study the patterns below closely, as **Lei** will use these verbs a lot.

Via
Cavour

(sah-peh-reh)
sapere
to know

Io _so/_ _____ tutto.
everything
(leen-dee-ree-tsoh)
Lei _sa/_ _____ l'indirizzo.
address

Lui _sa/_ _____ parlare italiano.
Lei (she)   to speak

Noi _sappiamo/_ _____ prendere il treno.

Loro _sanno/_ _____ parlare inglese.

Come
sta?

(poh-teh-reh)
potere
to be able to, can

Io _posso/_ _____ comprare un biglietto.

(kah-pee-reh)
Lei _può/_ _____ capire l'inglese.
understand
(moo-zeh-oh)
Lui _può/_ _____ vedere il museo.
Lei (she)

(jeh-oh-meh-tree-ah)
Noi _possiamo/_ imparare la geometria.

(mah-reh)
Loro _possono/_ _____ vedere il mare.
sea

(leh-jeh-reh)
leggere
to read

Io _____ il libro.

(jor-nah-leh)
Lei _____ il giornale.
newspaper

Lui _____ la lista.
Lei (she)   menu

Noi _leggiamo/_ _____ molto.
a lot

Loro _____ la rivista.
magazine

(doh-veh-reh)
dovere
to have to, must, to owe

(kohn-toh)
Io _devo/_ _____ pagare il conto.
bill

Lei _deve/_ _____ vedere il Colosseo.

Lui _deve/_ _____ scrivere due lettere.
Lei (she)

(lahl-bair-goh)
Noi _dobbiamo/_ _____ trovare l'albergo.

(vee-zee-tah-reh)
Loro _devono/_ _____ visitare Roma.
visit

❐ **il telefono** *(teh-leh-foh-noh)*	telephone	_____
❐ **il telegramma** *(teh-leh-grahm-mah)*	telegram	_____
❐ **il televisore** *(teh-leh-vee-zoh-reh)*	television set	**t** _____
❐ **la temperatura** *(tem-peh-rah-too-rah)*	temperature	_____
❐ **il Tevere** *(teh-veh-reh)*	Tiber River	_____

73

Notice that "**sapere**," "**dovere**," "**potere**," e "**vorrei**" can be combined with another verb.

Vorrei visitare Pisa.
(I) would like

Vorremmo bere due birre.
drink

Posso comprare un libro.
(I) can

Possiamo comprare una casa.

Devo visitare Roma.
(I) must

Dobbiamo pagare il conto.

Vorrei imparare l'italiano. *(eem-pah-rah-reh)*
(I) would like

Posso visitare Roma.
(I) can

Devo imparare l'italiano.
(I) must

So parlare italiano.
(I) know how to

Può you translate the sentences **qui sotto in italiano?** Le risposte sono qui sotto.
(pwoh) can
(kwee)
here

1. I know how to speak Italian. _____

2. They must pay the bill. _____

3. He has to pay the bill. _____

4. We know the address. _____ Sappiamo l'indirizzo. _____

5. She knows a lot. _____

6. We know how to read Italian. _____

7. I cannot find the hotel. _____

8. We do not understand French. _____

9. I would like to visit Rome. _____

10. She reads the newspaper. _____

LE RISPOSTE

1. So parlare italiano.
2. Devono pagare il conto.
3. Lui deve pagare il conto.
4. Sappiamo l'indirizzo.
5. Lei sa molto.
6. Sappiamo leggere l'italiano.
7. Non posso trovare l'albergo.
8. Non capiamo il francese.
9. Vorrei visitare Roma.
10. Lei legge il giornale.

Adesso, draw **linee** *(lee-neh-eh)* / lines **fra** the opposites **qui sotto. Non** forget to say them out loud. Use these

parole every day to describe **le cose nella Sua casa, nella Sua scuola** *(skoo-oh-lah)* / school **e nel Suo ufficio.**

(your home)

(grahn-deh)
grande

(see-nee-strah)
sinistra

(joh-vah-neh)
giovane

(poh-veh-roh)
povero

in buona *(sah-loo-teh)* **salute**

(loon-goh)
lungo

(mohl-toh)
molto

(bwoh-noh)
buono

(kee-oo-zoh)
chiuso

(soht-toh)
sotto

(kahl-doh)
caldo

(kah-roh)
caro

(len-toh)
lento

(soh-prah)
sopra

(kaht-tee-voh)
cattivo

(peek-koh-loh)
piccolo

(eh-koh-noh-mee-koh)
economico

(kor-toh)
corto

(mah-lah-toh)
malato

(ah-pair-toh)
aperto

(vek-kee-oh)
vecchio

(veh-loh-cheh)
veloce

(deh-strah)
destra

(poh-koh)
poco

(reek-koh)
ricco

(fred-doh)
freddo

❏ **la terrazza** *(tair-rah-tsah)*	terrace	
❏ **il tesoro** *(teh-zoh-roh)*	treasure	**t**
❏ **il titolo** *(tee-toh-loh)*	title	
❏ **la torre** *(tor-reh)*	tower	
— **La Torre Pendente**	Leaning Tower (of Pisa)	

(ee-eh-ree)
Ieri   a Venezia!
yesterday

(oh-jee)
Oggi a Firenze!
today

(doh-mah-nee)
Domani a Milano!
tomorrow

If you know a few key **parole,** traveling can be easy and quite efficient **in Italia. L'Italia non è**

grande, therefore **il viaggio è molto facile** within the distinctive "boot" **che si chiama**
(fah-chee-leh)   *(keh)* *(see)* *(kee-ah-mah)*
easy   that   is   called

"l'Italia." Come viaggiare in Italia?
(vee-ah-jah-reh)
to travel

Stefano viaggia in macchina.
(vee-ah-jah) *(mahk-kee-nah)*
travels   car

Franca viaggia in treno.

Francesca viaggia in aereo.
(ah-eh-reh-oh)
airplane

Anna viaggia in nave.
(nah-veh)
boat

Andrea viaggia in moto.
(moh-toh)

Silvia viaggia in autobus.

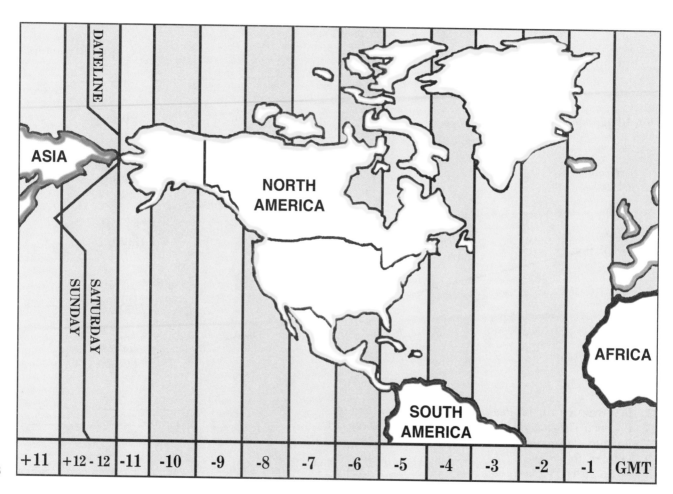

+11	+12 - 12	-11	-10	-9	-8	-7	-6	-5	-4	-3	-2	-1	GMT

Quando Lei are traveling, **Lei** will want to tell others your nationality **e Lei** will meet people from all corners of the world. Can you guess where people are from if they say one of the following? **Le risposte** are in your glossary beginning on page 108.

(een-gleh-zeh)
Sono inglese. —————————————
I am

(toor-koh)
Sono turco. —————————————
I am

(greh-kah)
Sono greca. —————————————
I am

(ah-oo-stree-ah-kah)
Sono austriaca. —————————————

(zveet-tsair-oh)
Sono svizzero. —————————————

(see-chee-lee-ah-nah)
Sono siciliana. —————————————

(ah-meh-ree-kah-noh)
Sono americano. —————————————

(kah-nah-deh-zeh)
Sono canadese. —————————————

(frahn-cheh-zee)
Siamo francesi. —————————————
we are

(teh-deh-skee)
Siamo tedeschi. —————————————
we are

(eer-lahnd-see)
Siamo irlandsi. —————————————

(ah-oo-strahl-ee-ah-nah)
Lei è australiana. —————————————
she   is

(jahp-poh-neh-zeh)
Lui è giaponese. —————————————
he   is

(roos-soh)
Lui è russo. —————————————

(sood-ah-free-kah-noh)
Lui è sudafricano. —————————————

(por-toh-geh-zeh)
Sono portoghese. —————————————

-1	GMT	+1	+2	+3	+4	+5	+6	+7	+8	+9	+10	+11	+12 -12

Gli Italiani enjoy going on *(vah-kahn-tseh)* **vacanze,** so it is no *(sor-preh-zah)* **sorpresa** to find **molte parole** built on **la**
(vee-ah-jah-reh)
parola "viaggiare," which means "to travel." Practice saying **le parole** *(seh-gwen-tee)* **seguenti** many times.
(spes-soh)
Lei will use them **spesso.**
often

(vee-ah-jah-reh)
viaggiare _____
to travel

(ah-jen-tsee-ah) *(vee-ah-jee)*
un'agenzia di viaggi _____
travel agency

(vee-ah-jah-toh-reh)
il viaggiatore _____
traveler

(bwohn) *(vee-ah-joh)*
Buon Viaggio! _____
have a good trip

If **Lei viaggia in macchina,** here are a few key **parole.**

(lah-oo-toh-strah-dah)
l'autostrada _____
freeway

(mahk-kee-nah) *(noh-leh-jah-reh)*
una macchina da noleggiare _____
rental car

(strah-dah)
la strada _____
street, road

(ah-jen-tsee-ah) *(noh-leh-joh)*
un'agenzia di noleggio _____
car rental agency

(par-kee-meh-troh)
il parchimetro _____
parking meter

(dee-skoh) *(soh-stah)*
il disco di sosta _____
parking disk

(chee)
Sotto ci sono some basic signs which **Lei** should also learn to recognize quickly.

(en-trah-reh)
entrare _____
to enter

(oo-shee-reh)
uscire _____
to exit

L'ENTRATA →

L'USCITA →

(len-trah-tah) *(leen-gres-soh)*
l'entrata or **l'ingresso**_____
entrance

(loo-shee-tah)
l'uscita _____
exit

(preen-chee-pah-leh)
l'entrata principale_____
main

(see-koo-reh-tsah)
l'uscita di sicurezza _____
emergency exit

SPINGERE

TIRARE

(speen-jeh-reh)
spingere _____
push (doors)

(tee-rah-reh)
tirare _____
pull (doors)

❐ **il tram** *(trahm)*	tram, street car	_____
❐ **tranquillo** *(trahn-kweel-loh)*	calm, tranquil	_____
❐ **tre** *(treh)*	three	_____
❐ **il treno** *(treh-noh)*	train	_____
❐ **il turista** *(too-ree-stah)*	tourist	_____

t

Let's learn the basic travel verbs. Take out a piece of paper **e** make up your own sentences with these **parole nuove.** Follow the same pattern as in previous Steps.

(ahn-dah-reh)　*(ah-eh-reh-oh)*
andare in aereo _____
to fly

(ar-ree-vah-reh)
arrivare _____
to arrive

(preh-noh-tah-reh)
prenotare _____
to reserve, to book

(cheh)　*(chee)*　*(soh-noh)*
c'è / ci sono _____
there is　　there are

(mahk-kee-nah)
andare in macchina _____
to drive

(par-tee-reh)
partire _____
to depart, to leave

(fah-reh)　*(vah-lee-jeh)*
fare le valige _____
to pack　　suitcases

(kahm-bee-ah-reh)
cambiare _____
to transfer (vehicles) or to change money!

Ecco some **parole nuove** per il **Suo** viaggio.
(soo-oh)
trip

(lah-eh-reh-oh-por-toh)
l'aereoporto
airport

(mar-chah-pee-eh-deh)　*(bee-nah-ree-oh)*
il marciapiede or **il binario**
platform　　　　　　train track

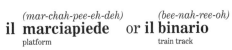

(loh-rah-ree-oh)
l'orario
timetable

Milano - Roma		
Partenza	**Treno**	**Arrivo**
00:41	50	09:41
07:40	19	15:40
12:15	22	00:15
14:32	10	23:32
21:40	04	09:40

(stah-tsee-oh-neh)
la stazione
train station

❏ **l'ufficio** *(loof-fee-choh)* .... office _____
❏ **ultimo** *(ool-tee-moh)* .... last, final, ultimate _____
❏ **unico** *(oo-nee-koh)* .... unique, only **u** _____
　— **senso unico** .... one-way (traffic) _____
❏ **universale** *(oo-nee-vair-sah-leh)* .... universal _____

Con these **parole, Lei è** ready for any **viaggio** *(vee-ah-joh)*, anywhere. **Lei** should have no problem **con**
_{are}

these new verbs, just remember the basic "plug-in" formula **Lei** have already learned. Use

that knowledge to translate the following thoughts **in italiano. Le risposte sono qui sotto.**
_{into}

1. I fly (go by plane) to Rome. _____

2. I transfer trains in Milan. _____

3. He drives to Padua. _____

4. We arrive tomorrow. _____

5. We buy tickets to Pisa. _____

6. They drive to Florence. _____

7. Where is the train to Trieste? _____

8. How can you fly (go by plane) to Italy? With American or with Alitalia? _____

Ecco some **parole importanti per il viaggiatore.** *(vee-ah-jah-toh-reh)*
_{traveler}

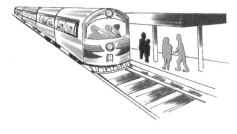

Bologna - Firenze		
Partenza	**Treno**	**Arrivo**
02:41	103	08:30
09:40	233	14:15
14:15	33	19:00
16:32	43	09:40
23:30	53	05:55

(ohk-koo-pah-toh)
occupato _____
occupied

(lee-beh-roh)
libero _____
free

(skohm-par-tee-men-toh)
lo scompartimento _____
compartment, wagon

(poh-stoh)
il posto _____
seat

(par-ten-tsah)
la partenza _____
departure

(lar-ree-voh)
l' arrivo _____
arrival

(een-tair-nah-tsee-oh-nah-leh)
internazionale _____
international

(nah-tsee-oh-nah-leh)
nazionale _____
domestic

Increase your travel **parole** by writing out **le parole qui** *(kwee)* **sotto e** practicing the sample sentences

out loud. Practice asking **domande con "dove."** It will help you later.

(pair)
per _____
to, for
                   Dov'è il treno per Roma?

(beel-yet-toh)
il biglietto _____
ticket
            Quanto costa un biglietto?

(loof-fee-choh) (oh-jet-tee) (zmar-ree-tee)
l'ufficio oggetti smarriti _____
lost-and-found office
        Dov'è l'ufficio oggetti smarriti?

(fahk-kee-noh)
il facchino _____
porter
          Dov'è il facchino?

(voh-loh)
il volo _____Dov'è il volo per Catania?_____
flight
          Dov'è il volo per Catania?

(deh-poh-zee-toh) (bah-gahl-yee)
il deposito bagagli _____
left-luggage office
        Dov'è un deposito bagagli?

(loof-fee-choh) (kahm-bee-oh)
l'ufficio di cambio _____
money-exchange office
        Dov'è l'ufficio di cambio?

(spor-tel-loh)
lo sportello _____
counter, ticket window
       Dov'è lo sportello numero otto?

(dah-spet-toh)
la sala d'aspetto _____
waiting room
       Dov'è la sala d'aspetto?

(vah-goh-neh) (ree-stoh-rahn-teh)
il vagone ristorante _____
dining car
       Dov'è il vagone ristorante?

(let-toh)
il vagone letto _____
sleeping car
       Dov'è il vagone letto numero due?

(foo-mah-reh)
fumare _____
to smoke
       È vietato fumare?
        prohibited

_____ **arriva il treno?**
(when)   (when)

_____ **è?**
(what)   (what) is it

(pwoh)
Può leggere le frasi seguenti?
can you   read   sentences following

(seh-doo-toh)
Lei è adesso seduto nell'aereo e Lei
                      seated

viaggia in Italia. Lei ha il denaro, il Suo

biglietto, il Suo passaporto e le Sue valige.
                                         suitcases

Adesso, è un turista. Lei arriva domani
              tourist

alle sei. Buon viaggio! Buon divertimento!

(loh-kah-leh)   *(dee-ret-toh)*

In Italia there are many different types of trains — **il treno locale è lento; il diretto è**
                                                 local   direct

rapido e both **il rapido e l'espresso** are **molto rapidi.** If **Lei** plan to travel a long distance, **Lei**

may wish to catch an Inter-City **treno o** a TEE or TEN train which travels faster **e** makes

fewer intermediate stops.

❑	**le vacanze** *(vah-kahn-tseh)*	vacation	_____
	— fare le vacanze	to go on vacation	_____
❑	**la vaccinazione** *(vah-chee-nah-tsee-oh-neh)* . .	vaccination **V**	_____
❑	**la vaniglia** *(vah-neel-yah)*	vanilla	_____
❑	**il vaporetto** *(vah-poh-ret-toh)*	steam ferry (in Venice)	_____

Knowing these travel **parole** will make your holiday twice as enjoyable **e** at least three times as easy. Review these **parole** by doing the crossword puzzle **qui sotto**. Drill yourself on this Step by selecting other destinations **e** ask your own **domande** about **i treni, gli autobus o gli aereoplani** that go there. Select **le parole nuove dal Suo dizionario e** ask your own questions beginning with **quando, dove, e quanto costa.** **Le risposte** to the crossword puzzle are at the bottom of the next page.

ACROSS
1. to rent (as in a car)
2. have a good trip
3. to smoke
4. occupied
5. timetable
6. money
7. foreigner
8. flight
9. nothing
10. time
11. street, road
12. to leave
13. arrival
14. entrance
15. station
16. to reserve
17. to go
18. domestic

DOWN
1. we / us
2. young
3. money-exchange
4. prohibited
5. track
6. exit
7. train
8. you (plural!)
9. ticket window
10. free
11. traveler
12. passport
13. departure

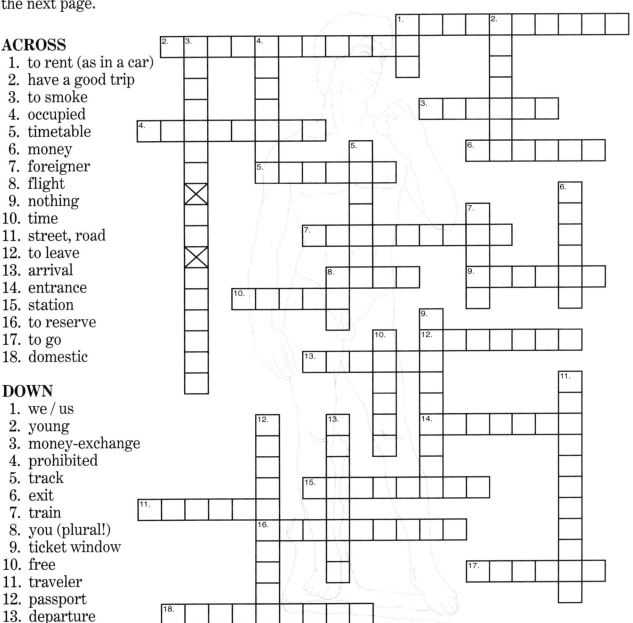

Davide – Michelangelo's famous figure dating from the 16th century. **Davide** is part of the collection of the Academy Gallery in Florence.

❏	**la varietà** *(vah-ree-eh-tah)*	variety	
❏	**il vaso** *(vah-zoh)*	vase	
❏	**la vena** *(veh-nah)*	vein **V**	
❏	**il venditore** *(ven-dee-toh-reh)*	vendor, seller	
❏	**la versione** *(vair-zee-oh-neh)*	version	

What about inquiring about **il prezzo dei biglietti?** *(preh-tsoh)* *(beel-yet-tee)* **Lei può** *(pwoh)* ask these **domande.**
price tickets can

(kwahn-toh)
Quanto costa un biglietto per Taranto? _____

Quanto costa un biglietto per Napoli? _____

Quanto costa un biglietto per Ravenna? _____

il biglietto di solo andata *(ahn-dah-tah)* _____
one-way ticket

il biglietto di andata e ritorno *(ahn-dah-tah)* *(ree-tor-noh)* _____
round trip ticket

What about times of **partenze e arrivi?** *(par-ten-tseh)* *(ar-ree-vee)* **Lei può** ask this as well.
departure arrival

A che ora parte il treno per Bari? *(keh)* *(par-teh)* _____
when departs for

A che ora arriva il treno da Parigi? *(ar-ree-vah)* *(pah-ree-jee)* _____

A che ora arriva l'aereo da New York? _____
arrives from

A che ora parte l'aereo per Roma? _____

A che ora parte il treno per Rimini? _____

Lei have just arrived **in Italia. Lei è alla stazione. Dove vorrebbe andare? A Lecce?** *(vor-reb-beh)*
would you like to go

A Orvieto? Tell that to the person at **lo sportello** selling **i biglietti!**
window

Vorrei andare a Siena. *(see-eh-nah)* _____
to go

A che ora parte il treno per Siena? _____

Quanto costa il biglietto per Siena? _____

LE RISPOSTE

ACROSS		DOWN	
1. noleggiare	7. straniero	1. noi	13. arrivo
2. buon viaggio	8. volo	2. giovane	14. entrata
3. fumare	9. niente	3. ufficio di cambio	15. stazione
4. occupato	10. tempo	4. vietato	16. prenotare
5. orario	11. strada	5. binario	17. andare
6. denaro	12. partire	6. uscita	18. nazionale
		7. treno	
		8. voi	
		9. sportello	
		10. libero	
		11. viaggiatore	
		12. passaporto	
		13. partenza	

Adesso that **Lei** know the essential words for traveling **in Italia** — what are some speciality items **Lei** might go in search of?

(pel-let-tair-ee-ah)
la pelletteria
leather goods

(joy-el-lee)
i gioielli
jewelry

(cheh-rah-mee-keh)
le ceramiche
pottery

(skar-peh)
le scarpe
shoes

(veh-stee-tee)
i vestiti
clothing

(proh-foo-mee)
i profumi
perfume

Consider using ITALIAN *a language map*® as well. ITALIAN *a language map*® is the perfect companion for your travels when **Lei** may not wish to take along this **libro**. Each section focuses on essentials for your **viaggio**. Your *Language Map*® is not meant to replace learning **italiano**, but will help you in the event **Lei** forget something and need a little bit of help. For more information, please turn to page 132 or go to www.bbks.com.

more information, please turn to page 132 or go to www.bbks.com.

❐ **la vergine** *(vair-jee-neh)*	virgin	
— **la Santa Vergine**	Holy Virgin	
❐ **la via** *(vee-ah); via*	way; by	**V**
— **via Appia Antica**	Appian Way	
— **via aerea**	by air, airmail	

Il Menù o La Lista
(meh-noo) *(lee-stah)*
menu

Adesso Lei è in Italia e Lei ha una camera. Lei ha fame. Dov'è un buon ristorante? First
(fah-meh)
hunger

of all, **ci sono** different types of places to eat. Let's learn them.
there are

(ree-stoh-rahn-teh)
il ristorante _____

exactly what it says with a variety of meals and prices

(traht-toh-ree-ah)
la trattoria _____

usually less elegant and less expensive than a **ristorante,** often run by a family

(loh-steh-ree-ah)
l'osteria _____

found in the country or in small towns, serves mostly drinks and easy-to-prepare food

(tah-voh-lah) *(kahl-dah)*
la tavola calda _____

similar to a cafeteria, with a variety of foods

il bar _____

serves pastries and sandwiches, concentrates on liquid refreshments
(great place for morning coffee or tea)

If **Lei** look around you **nel ristorante italiano, Lei** will see that some **costumi italiani** might
(koh-stoo-mee)
customs

be different from yours. Sharing **tavole con** others **è** a common **e molto** pleasant custom.

Before beginning your **pasto,** be sure to wish those sharing your table — **"Buon appetito!"**
(pah-stoh)   *(bwohn)* *(ahp-peh-tee-toh)*
meal   enjoy your meal

Your turn to practice now.

_____
(enjoy your meal)

And at least one more time for practice!

_____
(enjoy your meal)

❏ **vigoroso** *(vee-goh-roh-zoh)*	vigorous		_____
❏ **il vino** *(vee-noh)*	wine		_____
❏ **la visita** *(vee-zee-tah)*	visit	**v**	_____
— **fare una visita**	to pay a visit		_____
❏ **la vitamina** *(vee-tah-mee-nah)*	vitamin		

Start imagining now all the new taste treats you will experience abroad. Try all of the different

types of eating establishments. Experiment. If **Lei trova un ristorante** that **Lei** would like to

try, consider calling ahead to make a **prenotazione.** *(preh-noh-tah-tsee-oh-neh)* **"Vorrei fare una prenotazione."** If **Lei**

ha bisogno di una lista, catch the attention of **il cameriere,** *(kah-meh-ree-eh-reh)* ^{to make} by saying,

> **"Cameriere! La lista, per favore."**

_____
(Waiter! The menu, please.)

If your **cameriere** asks if **Lei** enjoyed your

pasto, a smile **e** a **"Sì, grazie"** will tell him

that you did.

Most **ristoranti italiani** post **la lista** outside **o** inside. Do not hesitate to ask to see **la lista**

before being seated so **Lei sa** what type of **pasti e prezzi Lei** will encounter. Most **ristoranti**
^{know} ^{meals} ^{prices}

offer **una lista a prezzo fisso.** *(preh-tsoh)* This is a complete **pasto** at a fair **prezzo.** Always look for the
^{fixed} ^{price}

piatto del giorno as well. *(pee-aht-toh) (jor-noh)*
^{daily special}

❑	**zero** *(zeh-roh)*	zero	_____
❑	**lo zodiaco** *(zoh-dee-ah-koh)*	zodiac	_____
	— **Sono del segno acquario**	I'm an Aquarius. **Z**	_____
❑	**la zona** *(zoh-nah)*	zone	_____
❑	**lo zoo** *(dzoh)*	zoo	_____

In Italia, ci sono tre main **pasti** *(pah-stee)* to enjoy every day, plus perhaps **un dolce** *(dohl-cheh)* **per** the tired

(vee-ah-jah-toh-reh) **viaggiatore** *(poh-meh-ree-joh)* **nel pomeriggio.**

there are *meals* *sweet* *for*

afternoon

(koh-lah-tsee-oh-neh)
la colazione / la prima colazione _____

breakfast

This meal usually consists of **caffè o tè e pane** or a sweet roll, butter and marmalade.

Check serving times before **Lei** retire for the night or you might miss out!

(prahn-tsoh)
il pranzo _____

mid-day meal

generally served from 12:00 to 14:00; this is the big meal of the day.

(cheh-nah)
la cena _____

evening meal

generally served from 19:30 to 22:00; this is a light meal.

Adesso for a preview of delights to come . . . At the back of this **libro, Lei** will find a sample

lista italiana. Legga la lista oggi e impari le parole nuove! When **Lei** are ready to leave

read *today* *learn*

on your **viaggio**, cut out **la lista**, fold it, **e** carry it in your pocket, wallet **o** purse. Before you go,

how do **Lei** say these **tre** phrases which are so very important for the hungry traveler?

Excuse me. I would like to make a reservation. _____

Waiter! The menu, please. _____

Enjoy your meal! _____

_____ *(mahn-jah)* **mangia l'insalata?** _____ **beve tè?**

(who) *eats* *(who)* *drinks*

_____ **viaggia a Venezia?**

(who)

Learning the following should help you to identify what kind of meat **Lei** have ordered **e come** it will be prepared.

☐ **il manzo** *(mahn-tsoh)* . . . . beef _____
☐ **il vitello** *(vee-tel-loh)* . . . . veal _____
☐ **il maiale** *(my-ah-leh)* . . . . pork _____
☐ **l'agnello** *(lahn-yel-loh)* . . . . lamb _____

Il menù below has the main categories **Lei** will find in most restaurants. Learn them **oggi** so that **Lei** will easily recognize them when you dine **a Roma, Siena o Ravenna.** Be sure to write the words in the blanks below.

(meh-noo)
Menù

(ahn-tee-pah-stee)
antipasti
appetizers

(zoop-peh)
zuppe
soups

(oo-oh-vah)
uova
eggs

(peh-sheh)
pesce
fish

(pee-aht-tee) *(jor-noh)*
piatti del giorno
daily specials

(pah-stah-shoot-tah)
pastasciutta
pasta

(ree-zoh)
riso
rice

(een-sah-lah-teh)
insalate
salads

(dohl-chee)
dolci
desserts

(vair-doo-rah)
verdura
vegetables

(froot-tah)
frutta
fruit

(for-mah-joh)
formaggio
cheese

(beh-vahn-deh)
bevande
beverages

❐ **il pollame** *(pohl-lah-meh)*	poultry	_____
❐ **il montone** *(mohn-toh-neh)*	mutton	_____
❐ **la cacciagione** *(kah-chah-joh-neh)*	game	_____
❐ **fritto** *(freet-toh)*	fried	_____
❐ **arrosto** *(ar-roh-stoh)*	roasted	

89

Lei may also order **verdura** *(vair-doo-rah)* **con il Suo pasto** or perhaps **un'insalata verde.** *(vair-deh)* One day at an open-air **mercato** *(mair-kah-toh)* will teach you **i nomi** for all the different kinds of **verdura e frutta,** *(froot-tah)* plus it will be a delightful experience for you. **Lei può** always consult your menu guide at the back of **questo libro** if **Lei** forget **il nome corretto. Adesso Lei** are seated **e il cameriere** arrives.

vegetables / green / mair-kah-toh / fruit / can / this / waiter

La lista, per favore.

E come bevanda?

Un bicchiere di vino bianco, per piacere.

La prima colazione è un po' differente *(poh)* because it is fairly standardized **e Lei** will frequently take it **nel Suo albergo** as **è generalmente** included **nel prezzo della Sua camera. Qui sotto c'è** a sample of what **Lei può** expect to greet you **la mattina.** *(maht-tee-nah)*

breakfast / a / little / in the morning

Bevande

caffè

tè

caffellatte
coffee and steamed milk

cioccolata

succo di arancia
juice / orange

succo di pomodoro
tomato

succo di pompelmo
grapefruit

latte

e . . .

pane

panino
roll

burro

marmellata
jam

prosciutto
ham

salsiccia
sausage

frittata
omelette

formaggio
cheese

❏ **cotto** *(koht-toh)*	cooked	_____
❏ **al forno** *(ahl)(for-noh)*	baked	_____
❏ **alla griglia** *(ahl-lah)(greel-yah)*	grilled	_____
❏ **farcito** *(far-chee-toh)*	stuffed	_____
❏ **bollito** *(bohl-lee-toh)*	boiled	_____

Ecco an example of what **Lei** might select for your evening meal. Using your menu guide on pages 117 and 118, as well as what **Lei** have learned in this Step, fill in the blanks *in English* with what **Lei** believe your **cameriere** will bring you. **Le risposte sono sotto.**

Antipasti
Antipasto misto

_____

Insalate
Insalata verde

_____

Piatto del Giorno
Vitello al pomodoro

_____

Dolci
Frutta di stagione

_____

(when)　　　　(how)　　　　(why)

LE RISPOSTE

Appetizers:	Assorted Appetizers
Salads:	Green salad
Entrees:	Veal in an Herbal Tomato Sauce
Desserts:	Seasonal Fruit

91

Adesso is a good time for a quick review. Draw lines between **le parole italiane e** their English equivalents.

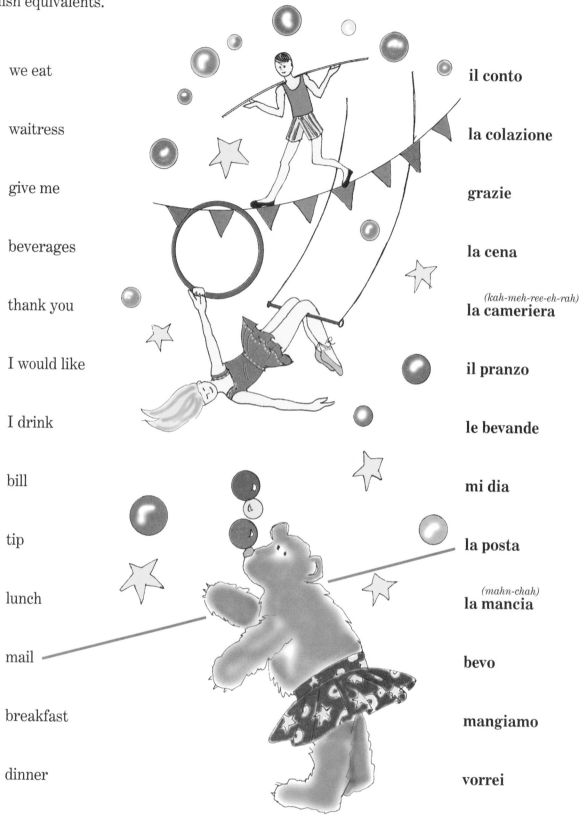

we eat

waitress

give me

beverages

thank you

I would like

I drink

bill

tip

lunch

mail

breakfast

dinner

il conto

la colazione

grazie

la cena

(kah-meh-ree-eh-rah)
la cameriera

il pranzo

le bevande

mi dia

la posta

(mahn-chah)
la mancia

bevo

mangiamo

vorrei

Ecco a few more holidays which you might experience during your visit.
- **Capodanno** *(kah-poh-dahn-noh)* . . . . New Year's Day
- **Festa della Resistenza** *(fes-tah)(del-lah)(reh-zee-sten-tsah)* . . . . Liberation Day
- **Pasqua** *(pah-skwah)* . . . . Easter
- **Festa del Lavoro** *(fes-tah)(del)(lah-voh-roh)* . . . . Labor Day

Che è differente about **il telefono in Italia?** Well, **Lei** never notice such things until **Lei** want

to use them. **I telefoni** allow you to call **amici,** *(ah-mee-chee)* reserve **i biglietti di teatro, di concerto o di**

balletto, *(bahl-let-toh)* make emergency calls, check on the hours of a **museo,** *(moo-zeh-oh)* rent **una macchina e** all those

other **cose** which **facciamo** *(fah-chah-moh)* on a daily basis. It also gives you a certain amount of **libertà**

we do

quando Lei può make your own **telefonate.** *(teh-leh-foh-nah-teh)*

calls

I telefoni can usually be found everywhere:

in the **ufficio postale,** on the **strada**, in the

bar, at the **stazione** and in the lobby of **il**

Suo albergo.

So, let's learn how to operate **il telefono.**

The instructions can look complicated,

but remember, some of these **parole**

Lei should be able to recognize already.

Ready? Well, before you turn the page

it would be a good idea to go back **e**

review all your numbers one more time.

To dial from the United States to most other countries **Lei** need that country's international area

code. Your **elenco** *(eh-len-koh)* **telefonico** at home should have a listing of international area codes.

telephone book

Ecco some very useful words built around the word **"telefono."**

- ❏ **la centralinista** *(chen-trah-lee-nee-stah)* . . . . operator
- ❏ **la cabina telefonica** *(kah-bee-nah)(teh-leh-foh-nee-kah)* . . . . public telephone booth
- ❏ **il telefonino / il cellulare** *(teh-leh-foh-nee-noh)/(chel-loo-lah-reh)* . . . . cellular telephone
- ❏ **la conversazione telefonica** *(kohn-vair-sah-tsee-oh-neh)(teh-leh-foh-nee-kah)* . . . . . . telephone conversation

When **Lei** leave your contact numbers with friends, family **e** business colleagues, **Lei** should include your destination's country code **e** city code whenever possible . For example,

	Country Codes		City Codes	
Italy	39	Rome	06
		Milan	02
		Venice	041
		Naples	081
Switzerland	41	Lugano	91

To call from one city to another city **in Italia,** you may need to go to **l'ufficio postale o** call **la centralinista** in your hotel. Tell **la centralinista,** "**Vorrei telefonare a Chicago**" **o**
operator

"**Vorrei telefonare a San Francisco.**"

Now you try it: _____
(I would like to call to . . . .)

When answering **il telefono,** pick up the receiver **e** say, " *(prohn-toh)* **Pronto! Sono** _____ ".
(your name)

When saying goodbye, say " **A domani**," or " *(ar-ree-veh-dair-chee)* **Arrivederci.**" Your turn —
until tomorrow   goodbye

_____
(Hello. This is . . .)

_____   _____
(goodbye)   (until tomorrow)

Non forget that **Lei può** ask . . .
can

Quanto costa telefonare *(nel-yee)* **negli** *(stah-tee)* **Stati** *(oo-nee-tee)* **Uniti?**_____
to call   to the   United States

Quanto costa telefonare a Firenze?_____
to call

Ecco free telephone calls.
☐ **in Italia:**   **polizia** *(poh-lee-tsee-ah)* . . . . police   113 _____
                     medico *(meh-dee-koh)* . . . . doctor   113 _____
☐ **in Svizzera:**   **polizia** *(poh-lee-tsee-ah)* . . . . police, help   117 _____
                     fuoco *(fwoh-koh)* . . . . fire brigade   118 _____

Ecco some sample sentences for **il telefono.** Write them in the blanks **sotto.**

Vorrei telefonare a Los Angeles. ⸻⸻⸻

Vorrei telefonare all'Alitalia all'aeroporto. ⸻⸻⸻

Vorrei telefonare a un medico. ⸻⸻⸻

(mee-oh)
Il mio numero è (06) 38-79-10-62. ⸻⸻⸻
my

(kwah-leh)
Qual'è il Suo numero di telefono? ⸻⸻⸻
what   is

Qual'è il numero di telefono dell'albergo? ⸻⸻⸻

Eva: **Pronto! Sono la signora Martini. Vorrei parlare con la Signora Rossi.**

⸻⸻⸻

Segretaria: **Un momento, per favore. Mi scusi, ma la linea è occupata.**
one   but

⸻⸻⸻

Eva: **Ripeta, per piacere.**
repeat

⸻⸻⸻

Segretaria: **Mi scusi, ma la linea è occupata.**

⸻⸻⸻

Eva: **Bene. Grazie. Arrivederci.**
well

⸻⸻⸻

Adesso Lei are ready to use any **telefono,** anywhere. Just take it **lentamente e** speak clearly.
(len-tah-men-teh)
slowly

Ecco countries **Lei** may wish to call.
- ❏ **Australia** *(ah-oo-strahl-yah)* . . . . Australia ⸻⸻
- ❏ **Austria** *(ah-oo-stree-ah)* . . . . Austria ⸻⸻
- ❏ **Egitto** *(eh-jeet-toh)* . . . . Egypt ⸻⸻
- ❏ **Inghilterra** *(een-gheel-tair-ah)* . . . . England ⸻⸻

(meh-troh)
Il metrò a Roma è a quick and cheap way to get around, though not as extensive as the
subway

(see-steh-mah)
sistema di autobus. A Roma, e in smaller cities, **c'è** *(sem-preh)* **sempre l'autobus**, which is slower, but
system   always

more scenic. **Lei** may also choose to go by *(tahs-see)* **tassì.**

(meh-troh)
il metrò
subway

(lah-oo-toh-boos)
l'autobus
bus

(fair-mah-tah)
la fermata del metrò
stop

(poh-steh-joh)
il posteggio dei tassì
parking place

(fair-mah-tah) (del-lah-oo-toh-boos)
la fermata dell'autobus
stop

Maps displaying the various *(lee-neh-eh)* **linee** **e** *(fair-mah-teh)* **fermate** **sono generalmente** posted outside every
lines   stops

(en-trah-tah)
entrata della stazione del metrò. Almost every *(pee-ahn-tah)* **pianta di Roma** also has a **metrò** map.
entrance   map

Le linee are color-coded to facilitate reading just like your example on the next page. If **Lei**
lines

deve cambiare treno or transfer to an **autobus,** look for **le** *(koh-een-chee-den-tseh)* **coincidenze** clearly marked at
must   connections

each **fermata.**

❏	**Francia** *(frahn-chah)*	France	_____
❏	**Germania** *(jair-mahn-yah)*	Germany	_____
❏	**Grecia** *(greh-chah)*	Greece	_____
❏	**Irlanda** *(eer-lahn-dah)*	Ireland	_____
❏	**Ungheria** *(oon-gair-ee-ah)*	Hungary	_____

Other than having foreign words, **il metrò italiano** functions just like in **New York o Londra.**

Locate your destination, select the correct line on your practice **metrò e** hop on board.

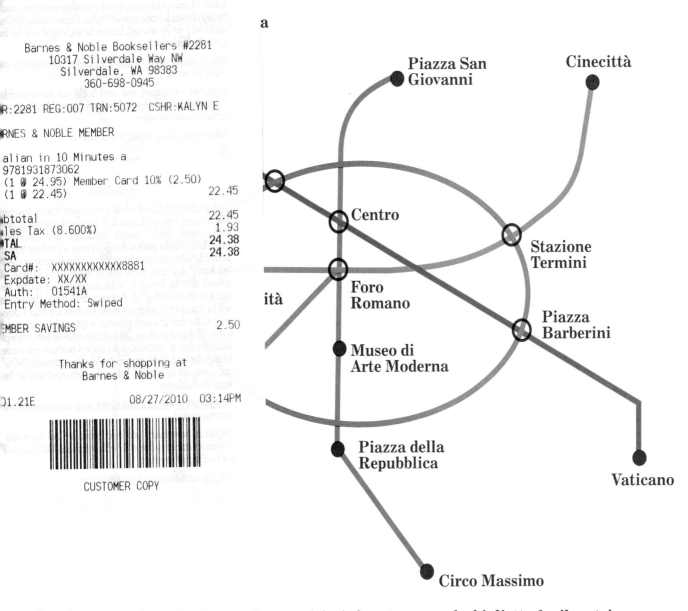

Say these questions aloud many times and don't forget you need a **biglietto** for **il metrò.**

Dov'è la fermata *(fair-mah-tah)* del metrò?

Dov'è la fermata dell'autobus?

Dov'è il posteggio dei tassì?

❏ **Portogallo** *(por-toh-gahl-loh)*	Portugal	_____
❏ **Spagna** *(spahn-yah)*	Spain	_____
❏ **Svizzera** *(zveet-tsair-ah)*	Switzerland	_____
❏ **Tunisia** *(too-nee-zee-ah)*	Tunisia	_____
❏ **Turchia** *(toor-kee-ah)*	Turkey	_____

Practice the following basic **domande** out loud **e** then write them in the blanks below.

1. *(ohn-yee)*
   Ogni quanto viene il metrò per il Colosseo? _____
   how often

   (vah-tee-kah-noh)
   Ogni quanto viene l'autobus per il Vaticano? _____

   Ogni quanto viene il treno per l'aeroporto? _____

2. *(kwahn-doh)*
   Quando parte il treno? _____
   when

   Quando parte l'autobus? _____ *Quando parte l'autobus?* _____

3. *(kwahn-toh) (koh-stah)   (beel-yet-toh)*
   Quanto costa un biglietto del metrò? _____

   Quanto costa un biglietto dell'autobus? _____

   (tah-reef-fah)
   Quant'è la tariffa? _____
   fare

4. **Dov'è la fermata del metrò?** _____

   Dov'è la fermata dell'autobus? _____

   (poh-steh-joh)
   Dov'è il posteggio dei tassì? _____

   (pohs-soh)
   Dove posso comprare un biglietto? _____
   can I

Let's change directions **e** learn **tre** new verbs. **Lei** know the basic "plug-in" formula, so

write out your own sentences using these new verbs.

(lah-vah-reh)
lavare _____
to wash

(or-dee-nah-reh)
ordinare _____
to order

(doo-rah-reh)
durare _____
to last

Ecco a few more holidays to keep in mind.
- ☐ **Ferragosto/Assunzione** *(fair-rah-goh-stoh)/(ahs-soon-tsee-oh-neh)* . . . . Assumption Day
- ☐ **Ognissanti** *(ohn-yees-sahn-tee)* . . . . All Saints' Day
- ☐ **L'Immacolata Concezione** *(leem-mah-koh-lah-tah)(kohn-cheh-tsee-oh-neh)* . . . . . . Immaculate Conception
- ☐ **Natale** *(nah-tah-leh)* . . . . Christmas

(ven-deh-reh) *(kohm-prah-reh)*

Vendere e Comprare
to sell   to buy

Shopping abroad is exciting. The simple everyday task of buying **un litro** *(lee-troh)* **di latte o una**
liter   milk

(meh-lah)
mela becomes a challenge that **Lei** should **adesso** be able to meet quickly **e** easily. Of course,
apple

Lei will purchase **dei** *(ree-kor-dee)* **ricordi, dei francobolli e delle cartoline** but **non** forget those many
souvenirs

(ah-spee-ree-nah)
other items ranging from shoelaces to **aspirina** that **Lei** might need unexpectedly. Locate
aspirin

your store, draw a line to it **e,** as always, write your new words in the blanks provided.

(mah-gah-tsee-noh)
il grande magazzino _____
department store

(chee-neh-mah)
il cinema _____
cinema

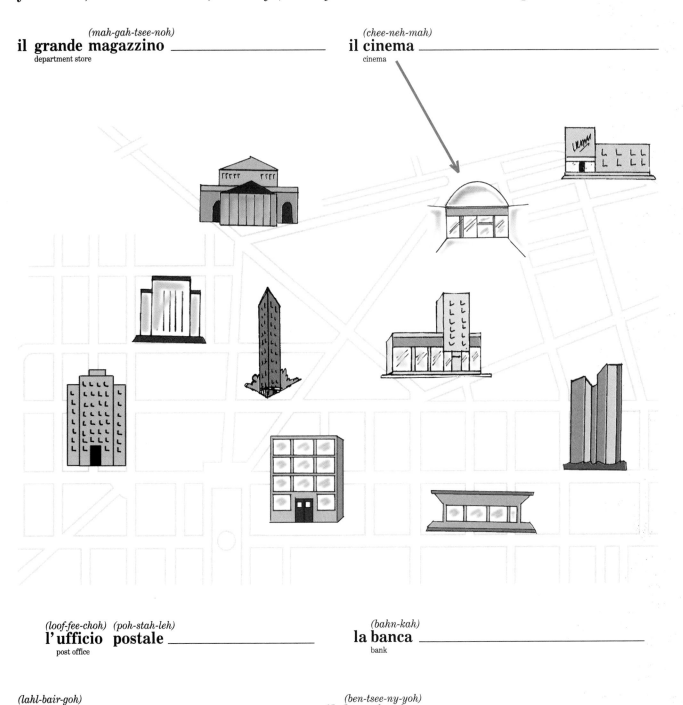

(loof-fee-choh) (poh-stah-leh)
l'ufficio postale _____
post office

(bahn-kah)
la banca _____
bank

(lahl-bair-goh)
l'albergo _____
hotel, inn

(ben-tsee-ny-yoh)
il benzinaio _____
gas station

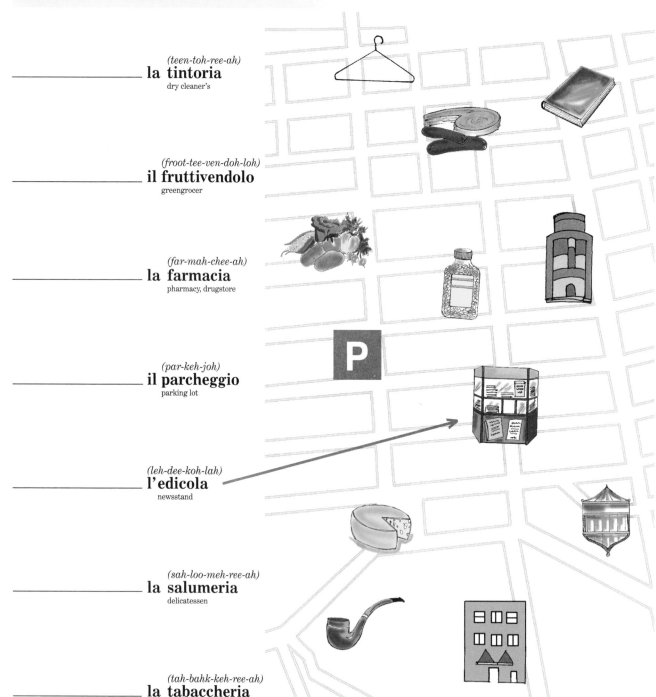

(neh-goh-tsee) *(ah-pair-tee)*
I negozi are generally **aperti** from
stores   open

9:00 until 18:30. Keep in mind, many shops

close for an extended lunch hour.

(mah-chel-leh-ree-ah)
la macelleria
butcher shop

_____

(lee-breh-ree-ah)
la libreria
bookstore

_____

(teen-toh-ree-ah)
_____ **la tintoria**
dry cleaner's

(froot-tee-ven-doh-loh)
_____ **il fruttivendolo**
greengrocer

(far-mah-chee-ah)
_____ **la farmacia**
pharmacy, drugstore

(par-keh-joh)
_____ **il parcheggio**
parking lot

(leh-dee-koh-lah)
_____ **l'edicola**
newsstand

(sah-loo-meh-ree-ah)
_____ **la salumeria**
delicatessen

(tah-bahk-keh-ree-ah)
_____ **la tabaccheria**
tobacco shop

Local, open-air **mercati sono** truly
(oo-neh-speh-ree-en-tsah)   *(oh-reh)*
un'esperienza, so be sure to check **le ore**
experience   hours

of the one closest to **il Suo albergo.**

(lah-jen-tsee-ah) *(vee-ah-jee)*
l'agenzia di viaggi
travel agency

_____

(poh-lee-tsee-ah)
la polizia
police

_____

(laht-teh-ree-ah)
la latteria
dairy

(fee-oh-rye-yoh)
il fioraio
florist

(peh-skeh-ree-ah)
la pescheria _____
fish store

(loht-tee-koh)
l'ottico _____
camera store

(mair-kah-toh)
il mercato _____
market

(soo-pair-mair-kah-toh)
il supermercato _____
supermarket

(loh-roh-loh-jeh-ree-ah)
l' orologeria _____
clock and watchmaker's shop

(pah-net-teh-ree-ah)
la panetteria _____
bakery

(pah-stee-cheh-ree-ah)
la pasticceria _____
pastry shop

(lah-vahn-deh-ree-ah)
la lavanderia _____
laundromat

(kar-toh-leh-ree-ah)
la cartoleria
stationery store

(par-rook-kee-eh-reh)
il parrucchiere
hairdresser

In Italia, the ground floor is called "il

(pee-ahn-tair-reh-noh)
pianterreno." The first floor (**primo**

piano) **è** the next floor up **e** so on.

(grahn-deh) *(mah-gah-tsee-noh)*

Il Grande Magazzino
department store

At this point, **Lei** should just about be ready for **il Suo viaggio. Lei** have gone shopping for those last-minute odds 'n ends. Most likely, the store directory at your local **grande magazzino** *(mah-gah-tsee-noh)* did not look like the one **sotto. Lei sa che "bambino"** *(bahm-bee-noh)* is Italian for "<u>child</u>" so if **Lei ha bisogno di** something for a child, **Lei** would probably look on the **secondo o terzo piano, vero?**

know

4.■ PIANO	cristalleria vasellame da cucina alimentari verdura	servizi da tavola mobili da cucina tavola calda salumeria	chiavi ceramica porcellana frutta
3.■ PIANO	libri televisori mobili da bambini giocattoli	radio strumenti musicali cartoleria dischi	ristorante giornali riviste vino
2.■ PIANO	tutto per il bambino vestiti da donna cappelli da donna specchi	vestiti da uomo scarpe da bambino foto lampade	gabinetti antiquario tappeti mobili

1.■ PIANO	accessori da
	   macchina
	fazzoletti
	biancheria
		costumi da bagno
		scarpe da donna
		scarpe da uomo
			articoli sportivi
			articoli da
			   campeggio
			ferramenta

P	ombrelli biglietti di auguri cappelli da uomo gioielleria	guanti articoli di pelle e cuoio calze	cinture orologi profumeria pasticceria

Let's start a checklist **per il Suo viaggio.** Besides **vestiti,** *(veh-stee-tee)* **di che ha bisogno?** *(keh)* *(bee-zohn-yoh)* As you learn

clothing   what do you need

these **parole,** assemble these items **in un angolo** *(ahn-goh-loh)* of your **casa.** Check **e** make sure that they

corner

sono puliti *(poo-lee-tee)* **e** ready **per il Suo viaggio.** Be sure to do the same **con** the rest of **le cose** that

clean   with   things

Lei pack. On the next pages, match each item to its picture, draw a line to it and write out the word many times. As **Lei** organize these things, check them off on this list. Do not forget to take the next group of sticky labels and label these **cose oggi.** *(oh-jee)*

today

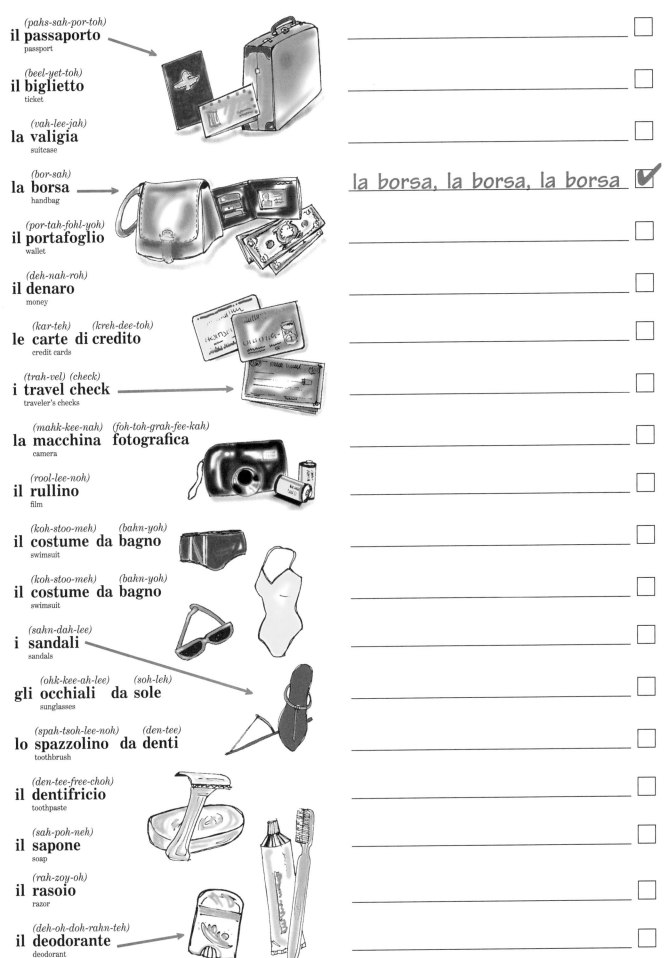

il passaporto *(pahs-sah-por-toh)*
passport

il biglietto *(beel-yet-toh)*
ticket

la valigia *(vah-lee-jah)*
suitcase

la borsa *(bor-sah)*
handbag

la borsa, la borsa, la borsa ✓

il portafoglio *(por-tah-fohl-yoh)*
wallet

il denaro *(deh-nah-roh)*
money

le carte di credito *(kar-teh) (kreh-dee-toh)*
credit cards

i travel check *(trah-vel) (check)*
traveler's checks

la macchina fotografica *(mahk-kee-nah) (foh-toh-grah-fee-kah)*
camera

il rullino *(rool-lee-noh)*
film

il costume da bagno *(koh-stoo-meh) (bahn-yoh)*
swimsuit

il costume da bagno *(koh-stoo-meh) (bahn-yoh)*
swimsuit

i sandali *(sahn-dah-lee)*
sandals

gli occhiali da sole *(ohk-kee-ah-lee) (soh-leh)*
sunglasses

lo spazzolino da denti *(spah-tsoh-lee-noh) (den-tee)*
toothbrush

il dentifricio *(den-tee-free-choh)*
toothpaste

il sapone *(sah-poh-neh)*
soap

il rasoio *(rah-zoy-oh)*
razor

il deodorante *(deh-oh-doh-rahn-teh)*
deodorant

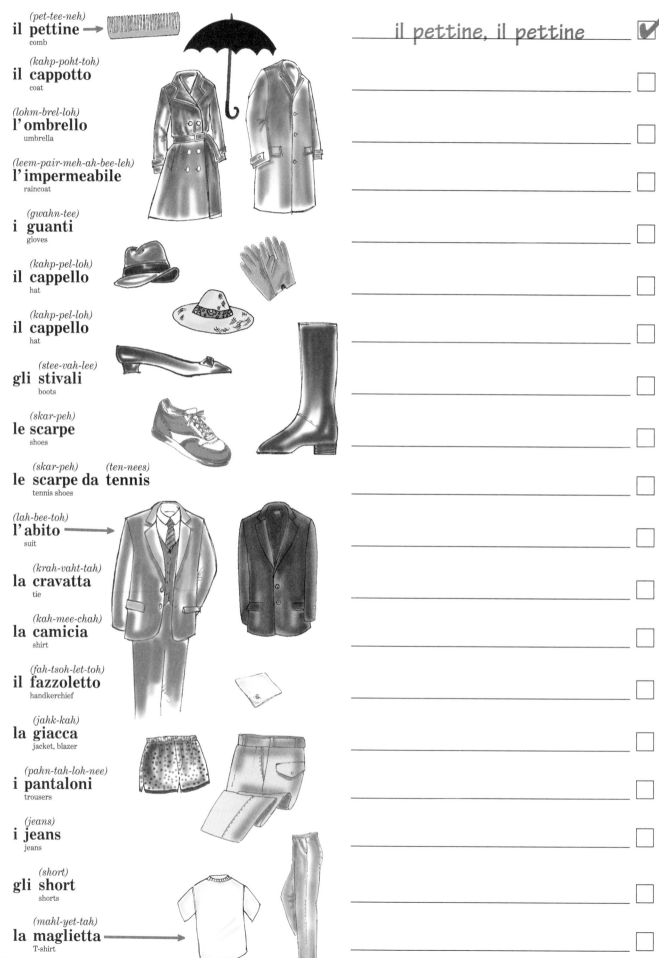

(pet-tee-neh)
il pettine
comb

(kahp-poht-toh)
il cappotto
coat

(lohm-brel-loh)
l'ombrello
umbrella

(leem-pair-meh-ah-bee-leh)
l'impermeabile
raincoat

(gwahn-tee)
i guanti
gloves

(kahp-pel-loh)
il cappello
hat

(kahp-pel-loh)
il cappello
hat

(stee-vah-lee)
gli stivali
boots

(skar-peh)
le scarpe
shoes

(skar-peh) *(ten-nees)*
le scarpe da tennis
tennis shoes

(lah-bee-toh)
l'abito
suit

(krah-vaht-tah)
la cravatta
tie

(kah-mee-chah)
la camicia
shirt

(fah-tsoh-let-toh)
il fazzoletto
handkerchief

(jahk-kah)
la giacca
jacket, blazer

(pahn-tah-loh-nee)
i pantaloni
trousers

(jeans)
i jeans
jeans

(short)
gli short
shorts

(mahl-yet-tah)
la maglietta
T-shirt

il pettine, il pettine ✔

(moo-tahn-deh)
le mutande
underpants

(kah-noht-tee-eh-rah)
la canottiera
undershirt

(veh-stee-toh)
il vestito
dress

(kah-mee-chet-tah)
la camicetta
blouse

(gohn-nah)
la gonna
skirt

la gonna, la gonna, la gonna ✔

(gohl-fee-noh)
il golfino
sweater

(soht-toh-veh-steh)
la sottoveste
slip

(reh-jee-pet-toh)
il reggipetto
brassiere

(moo-tahn-dee-neh)
le mutandine
underpants

(kahl-tsee-nee)
i calzini
socks

(kahl-tseh)
le calze
pantyhose

(pee-jah-mah)
il pigiama
pajamas

(kah-mee-chah) *(noht-teh)*
la camicia da notte
nightshirt

(lahk-kahp-pah-toy-oh)
l'accappatoio
bathrobe

(pahn-toh-foh-leh)
le pantofole
slippers

From now on, **Lei ha il** *(sah-poh-neh)* **"sapone" e non** "soap." Having assembled these **cose, Lei** are ready
have   things

viaggiare. Let's add these important shopping phrases to your basic repertoire.
to travel

(keh) *(tahl-yah)*
Che taglia? _____
what   size

(mee) *(vah)*
Questo mi va bene. _____
this fits me

Questo non mi va bene. _____
this does not fit me

Treat yourself to a final review. **Lei sa** the names for **i negozi** *(neh-goh-tsee)* **italiani,** so let's practice

shopping. Just remember your key question **parole** that you learned in Step 2. Whether **Lei**

need to buy **ricordi** *(ree-kor-dee)* **o libri** the necessary **parole** are the same.
souvenirs

1. First step — **Dove?**

Dov'è la latteria?   **Dov'è la banca?**   **Dov'è il fioraio?** *(fee-oh-rye-yoh)*   **Dov'è il cinema?** *(chee-neh-mah)*

_____

(Where is the department store?)

_____

(Where is the grocery store?)

_____

(Where is the market?)

2. Second step — tell them what **Lei** are looking for, need **o vorrebbe.**

Ho bisogno di . . .   **Vorrei . . .**   **Lei ha . . . ?**
I need   I would like   do you have

_____

(Do you have postcards?)

_____

(I would like four stamps.)

_____

(I need toothpaste.)

_____

(I would like to buy film.)

_____

(Do you have coffee?)

Go through the glossary at the end of this **libro e** select **venti parole.** Drill the above patterns **con** these twenty **parole.** Don't cheat. Drill them *(oh-jee)* **oggi. Adesso,** take **venti** more **parole dal Suo** glossary **e** do the same.

3. Third step — find out *(kwahn-toh)* **quanto costa.**

Quant'è?	*(frahn-koh-bohl-loh)* **Quanto costa un francobollo?**	**Quanto costa una cartolina?**

_____

(How much does the toothpaste cost?)

_____

(How much does the soap cost?)

_____

(How much does a cup of tea cost?)

4. Fourth step — success! I found it!

Once **Lei** find what **Lei** would like, **Lei** *(dee-cheh)* **dice,** say

(kwes-toh) **Vorrei questo, per favore.** _____ *Vorrei questo, per favore.* _____
that

or

Mi dia questo, per favore. _____
give me

O if **Lei** would not like it, **Lei dice,**

(vohl-yoh) **Non lo voglio, grazie.** _____
I do not want it

or

(mee) (pee-ah-cheh) **Non mi piace.** _____
I do not like it

Congratulations! You have finished. By now you should have stuck your labels, flashed your cards, cut out your menu guide and packed your suitcases. You should be very pleased with your accomplishment. You have learned what it sometimes takes others years to achieve and you hopefully had fun doing it. **Buon viaggio!**

Glossary

This glossary contains words used in this book only. It is not meant to be a dictionary. Consider purchasing a dictionary which best suits your needs - small for traveling, large for reference, or specialized for specific vocabulary needs.

The words here are all presented in alphabetical order followed by the pronunciation guide used in this book.

Remember that Italian words can change their endings depending upon how they are used. Not all variations are given here. If you need a refresher on how to make a noun plural or how to change an adjective from masculine to feminine, refer to page 49.

A

a *(ah)* . . . . at, to
a domani *(ah)(doh-mah-nee)* . . . . until tomorrow
abbiamo *(ahb-bee-ah-moh)* . . . . we have
abitare *(ah-bee-tah-reh)* . . . . to live, to reside
abito, l' *(ah-bee-toh)* . . . . suit
accanto a *(ahk-kahn-toh)(ah)* . . . . next to
accappatoio, l' *(ahk-kahp-pah-toy-oh)* . . . . bathrobe
accettare *(ah-chet-tah-reh)* . . . . to accept
acqua, l' *(ah-kwah)* . . . . water
adesso *(ah-des-soh)* . . . . now
aereo, l' *(ah-eh-reh-oh)* . . . . airplane
aereoporto, l' *(ah-eh-roh-por-toh)* . . . . airport
agenzia di noleggio, l' *(ah-jen-tsee-ah)(dee)(noh-leh-joh)* . . . . .
. . . . car rental agency
agenzia di viaggi, l' *(ah-jen-tsee-ah)(dee)(vee-ah-jee)* . . . .
. . . . travel agency
agnello, l' *(ahn-yel-loh)* . . . . lamb
agosto *(ah-goh-stoh)* . . . . August
aiuto *(eye-oo-toh)* . . . . help
al forno *(ahl)(for-noh)* . . . . baked
albergatore, l' *(ahl-bair-gah-toh-reh)* . . . . hotelkeeper
albergo, l' *(ahl-bair-goh)* . . . . hotel
alcool, l' *(ahl-kohl)* . . . . alcohol
alfabeto, l' *(ahl-fah-beh-toh)* . . . . alphabet
al *(ahl)* . . . . to the, at the
alla *(ahl-lah)* . . . . to the, at the
alla griglia *(ahl-lah)(greel-yah)* . . . . grilled
alle *(ahl-leh)* . . . . at the, at
allo *(ahl-loh)* . . . . to the, at the
Alpi, le *(ahl-pee)* . . . . Alps
alto *(ahl-toh)* . . . . tall
America, l' *(ah-meh-ree-kah)* . . . . America
americano, l' *(ah-meh-ree-kah-noh)* . . . . American
amico, l' *(ah-mee-koh)* . . . . friend
anche *(ahn-keh)* . . . . also
ancora *(ahn-koh-rah)* . . . . more, still
andare *(ahn-dah-reh)* . . . . to go
andare in aereo *(ahn-dah-reh)(een)(ah-eh-reh-oh)* . . . . . . to fly
andare in macchina *(ahn-dah-reh)(een)(mahk-kee-nah)* . . to drive
andata e ritorno *(ahn-dah-tah)(eh)(ree-tor-noh)* . . . round-trip
angolo, l' *(ahn-goh-loh)* . . . . corner
animale, l' *(ah-nee-mah-leh)* . . . . animal
antipasti, gli *(ahn-tee-pah-stee)* . . . . appetizers
aperto *(ah-pair-toh)* . . . . open
appartamento, l' *(ahp-par-tah-men-toh)* . . . . apartment
appuntamenti, gli *(ahp-poon-tah-men-tee)* . . . . . appointments
aprile *(ah-pree-leh)* . . . . April
aprire *(ah-pree-reh)* . . . . to open
arancione *(ah-rahn-choh-neh)* . . . . orange (color)
armadietto, l' *(ar-mah-dee-et-toh)* . . . . cupboard
armadio, l' *(ar-mah-dee-oh)* . . . . wardrobe

arriva *(ar-ree-vah)* . . . . arrive, arrives
arrivare *(ar-ree-vah-reh)* . . . . to arrive
arrivederci *(ar-ree-veh-dair-chee)* . . . . goodbye
arrivo, l' *(ah-ree-voh)* . . . . arrival
arrosto *(ar-roh-stoh)* . . . . roasted
asciugamani, gli *(ah-shoo-gah-mah-nee)* . . . . towels
aspettare *(ah-spet-tah-reh)* . . . . to wait (for)
aspirina, l' *(ah-spee-ree-nah)* . . . . aspirin
attenzione, l' *(aht-ten-tsee-oh-neh)* . . . . attention
attore, l' *(aht-toh-reh)* . . . . actor
Australia, l' *(ah-oo-strahl-yah)* . . . . Australia
Austria, l' *(ah-oo-stree-ah)* . . . . Austria
austriaco, *(ah-oo-stree-ah-koh)* . . . . Austrian
auto, l' *(ah-oo-toh)* . . . . car
autobus, l' *(ah-oo-toh-boos)* . . . . bus
autostrada, l' *(ah-oo-toh-strah-dah)* . . . . highway, freeway
autunno, l' *(ah-oo-toon-noh)* . . . . autumn
avere *(ah-veh-reh)* . . . . to have
avere bisogno di *(ah-veh-reh)(bee-zohn-yoh)(dee)* . . . . . to need

B

bagno, il *(bahn-yoh)* . . . . bathroom
baia, la *(bah-ee-ah)* . . . . bay
balcone, il *(bahl-koh-neh)* . . . . balcony
balletto, il *(bahl-let-toh)* . . . . ballet
bambino, il *(bahm-bee-noh)* . . . . child
banana, la *(bah-nah-nah)* . . . . banana
banca, la *(bahn-kah)* . . . . bank
bancomat, il *(bahn-koh-maht)* . . . . ATM
bar, il *(bar)* . . . . bar, pub, café
basso *(bahs-soh)* . . . . short
bello *(bel-loh)* . . . . nice, beautiful
bene *(beh-neh)* . . . . good, well
benedizione, la *(beh-neh-dee-tsee-oh-neh)* . . . . benediction
benzina, la *(ben-tsee-nah)* . . . . gas
benzinaio, il *(ben-tsee-ny-yoh)* . . . . gas station
bere *(beh-reh)* . . . . to drink
bevande, le *(beh-vahn-deh)* . . . . beverages
bianco *(bee-ahn-koh)* . . . . white
bicchiere, il *(beek-kee-eh-reh)* . . . . glass
bicchiere di vino, il *(beek-kee-eh-reh)(dee)(vee-noh)* . . . .
. . . . wine glass
bici, la *(bee-chee)* . . . . bicycle
bicicletta, la *(bee-chee-klet-tah)* . . . . bicycle
biglietto, il *(beel-yet-toh)* . . . . bank note, bill, ticket
binario, il *(bee-nah-ree-oh)* . . . . train track
birra, la *(beer-rah)* . . . . beer
biscotto, il *(bee-skoht-toh)* . . . . biscuit, cookie
bisogno, il *(bee-zohn-yoh)* . . . . need
bistecca, la *(bee-stek-kah)* . . . . steak
blu *(bloo)* . . . . blue
bollito *(bohl-lee-toh)* . . . . boiled

borsa, la *(bor-sah)* . . . . handbag, purse
bottiglia, la *(boht-teel-yah)* . . . . bottle
breve *(breh-veh)* . . . . brief, short
brillante *(breel-lahn-teh)* . . . . shining, brilliant
brutto *(broot-toh)* . . . . bad
buca delle lettere, la *(boo-kah)(del-leh)(let-teh-reh)* . . . mailbox
buon, buona, buono *(bwohn)(bwoh-nah)(bwoh-noh)* . . . . . good
  buon appetito *(bwohn)(ahp-peh-tee-toh)* . . . enjoy your meal
  buon divertimento *(bwohn)(dee-vair-tee-men-toh)* . . . have fun
  buona fortuna *(bwoh-nah)(for-too-nah)* . . . . good luck
  buon giorno *(bwohn)(jor-noh)* . . . . . good morning, good day
  buona notte *(bwoh-nah)(noht-teh)* . . . . good night
  buona sera *(bwoh-nah)(seh-rah)* . . . . good evening
  buon viaggio *(bwohn)(vee-ah-joh)* . . . . Have a good trip!
burro, il *(boor-roh)* . . . . butter

C

cabina telefonica, la *(kah-bee-nah)(teh-leh-foh-nee-kah)* . . . . .
. . . . telephone booth
cacciagione, la *(kah-chah-joh-neh)* . . . . wild game
caffè, il *(kahf-feh)* . . . . coffee
caldo *(kahl-doh)* . . . . warm, hot
calendario, il *(kah-len-dah-ree-oh)* . . . . calendar
calze, le *(kahl-tseh)* . . . . pantyhose
calzino, il *(kahl-tsee-noh)* . . . . sock
cambiare *(kahm-bee-ah-reh)* . . . .
. . . . to transfer (vehicles), to change (money)
camera, la *(kah-meh-rah)* . . . . room
  camera doppia, la *(kah-meh-rah)(dohp-pyah)* . . double room
  camera singola, la *(kah-meh-rah)(seen-goh-lah)* . . single room
  camera da letto, la *(kah-meh-rah)(dah)(let-toh)* . . . . bedroom
cameriera, la *(kah-meh-ree-eh-rah)* . . . . waitress
cameriere, il *(kah-meh-ree-eh-reh)* . . . . waiter
camicetta, la *(kah-mee-chet-tah)* . . . . blouse
camicia, la *(kah-mee-chah)* . . . . shirt
camicia da notte, la *(kah-mee-chah)(dah)(noht-teh)* . . nightshirt
Canada, il *(kah-nah-dah)* . . . . Canada
canadese *(kah-nah-deh-zeh)* . . . . Canadian
cane, il *(kah-neh)* . . . . dog
canottiera, la *(kah-noht-tee-eh-rah)* . . . . undershirt
cantina, la *(kahn-tee-nah)* . . . . cellar, basement
capire *(kah-pee-reh)* . . . . to understand
capitale, la *(kah-pee-tah-leh)* . . . . capital
Capodanno *(kah-poh-dahn-noh)* . . . . New Year's Day
cappello, il *(kahp-pel-loh)* . . . . hat
cappotto, il *(kahp-poht-toh)* . . . . coat
carne, la *(kar-neh)* . . . . meat
caro *(kah-roh)* . . . . expensive
  è troppo caro *(eh)(trohp-poh)(kah-roh)* . . . (it) is too expensive
carta, la *(kar-tah)* . . . . paper, map
carta di credito, la *(kar-tah)(dee)(kreh-dee-toh)* . . . . credit card
cartoleria, la *(kar-toh-leh-ree-ah)* . . . . stationery store
cartolina, la *(kar-toh-lee-nah)* . . . . postcard
casa, la *(kah-zah)* . . . . house
cassa, la *(kahs-sah)* . . . . cashier's desk
castello, il *(kah-stel-loh)* . . . . castle
categoria, la *(kah-teh-goh-ree-ah)* . . . . category
cattedrale, la *(kaht-teh-drah-leh)* . . . . cathedral
cattivo *(kaht-tee-voh)* . . . . bad
cattolico *(kaht-toh-lee-koh)* . . . . Catholic
c'è *(cheh)* . . . . it is, there is
cellulare, il *(chel-loo-lah-reh)* . . . . cellular telephone
cena, la *(cheh-nah)* . . . . dinner
Centigrado *(chen-tee-grah-doh)* . . . . Centigrade
cento *(chen-toh)* . . . . one hundred
centralinista, la *(chen-trah-lee-strah)* . . . . . telephone operator
centro, il *(chen-troh)* . . . . center, downtown

ceramiche, le *(cheh-rah-mee-keh)* . . . . pottery
cerimonia, la *(cheh-ree-moh-nee-ah)* . . . . ceremony
certo *(chair-toh)* . . . . certainly
cestino, il *(cheh-stee-noh)* . . . . wastebasket
che *(keh)* . . . . what
chi *(kee)* . . . . who
chiamarsi *(kee-ah-mar-see)* . . . . to be called
chiesa, la *(kee-eh-zah)* . . . . church
chiuso *(kee-oo-zoh)* . . . . closed
ci sono *(chee)(soh-noh)* . . . . there are
ciao *(chow)* . . . . hi! / bye!
cifra, la *(cheef-rah)* . . . . figure, number
cinema, il *(chee-neh-mah)* . . . . cinema, movie house
cinese, il *(chee-neh-zeh)* . . . . Chinese
cinquanta *(cheen-kwahn-tah)* . . . . fifty
cinque *(cheen-kweh)* . . . . five
cinquecento *(cheen-kweh-chen-toh)* . . . . five hundred
cioccolato, il *(chohk-koh-lah-toh)* . . . . chocolate
coincidenza, la *(koh-een-chee-den-tsah)* . . . . . . train connection
colazione, la *(koh-lah-tsee-oh-neh)* . . . . breakfast, lunch
colore, il *(koh-loh-reh)* . . . . color
coltello, il *(kohl-tel-loh)* . . . . knife
come *(koh-meh)* . . . . how
  Come sta? *(koh-meh)(stah)* . . . . How are you?
comincia *(koh-meen-chah)* . . . . commences, begins
comprare *(kohm-prah-reh)* . . . . to buy
computer, il *(kohm-pyoo-tair)* . . . . computer
comunicazione, la *(koh-moo-nee-kah-tsee-oh-neh)* . . . .
. . . . communication
con *(kohn)* . . . . with
concerto, il *(kohn-chair-toh)* . . . . concert
conservazione, la *(kohn-sair-vah-tsee-oh-neh)* . . . conservation
continui *(kohn-tee-noo-ee)* . . . . continue
conto, il *(kohn-toh)* . . . . bill
conversazione, la *(kohn-vair-sah-tsee-oh-neh)* . . . conversation
coperta, la *(koh-pair-tah)* . . . . blanket
coraggio, il *(koh-rah-joh)* . . . . courage
corretto *(kor-ret-toh)* . . . . correct
corto *(kor-toh)* . . . . short
cosa, la *(koh-zah)* . . . . thing
costa *(koh-stah)* . . . . (it) costs
costare *(koh-stah-reh)* . . . . to cost
costume, il *(koh-stoo-meh)* . . . . custom
costume da bagno, il *(koh-stoo-meh)(dah)(bahn-yoh)* . . . .
. . . . swimsuit
cotto *(koht-toh)* . . . . cooked
cravatta, la *(krah-vaht-tah)* . . . . tie
cucchiaio, il *(kook-kee-eye-oh)* . . . . spoon
cucina, la *(koo-chee-nah)* . . . . kitchen, stove
cugina, la *(koo-jee-nah)* . . . . female cousin
cugino, il *(koo-jee-noh)* . . . . male cousin
cuscino, il *(koo-shee-noh)* . . . . pillow

D

da *(dah)* . . . . from
dagli *(dahl-yee)* . . . . from the
dal *(dahl)* . . . . from the
dalla *(dahl-lah)* . . . . from the
danza, la *(dahn-tsah)* . . . . dance
davanti a *(dah-vahn-tee)(ah)* . . . . in front of
decorato *(deh-koh-rah-toh)* . . . . decorated
degli *(del-yee)* . . . . some, of the
dei *(deh-ee)* . . . . some, of the
del, della, delle *(del)(del-lah)(del-leh)* . . . . some, of the
delizioso *(deh-lee-tsee-oh-zoh)* . . . . delicious

109

denaro, il *(deh-nah-roh)* . . . . money
denso *(den-soh)* . . . . dense
dentifricio, il *(den-tee-free-choh)* . . . . toothpaste
deodorante, il *(deh-oh-doh-rahn-teh)* . . . . deodorant
deposito bagagli, il *(deh-poh-zee-toh)(bah-gahl-yee)* . . . .
. . . . left-luggage office
desiderio, il *(deh-zee-deh-ree-oh)* . . . . desire, wish
destra *(deh-strah)* . . . . right
deviazione, la *(deh-vee-ah-tsee-oh-neh)* . . . . detour
di *(dee)* . . . . of, in
dicembre *(dee-chem-breh)* . . . . December
diciannove *(dee-chahn-noh-veh)* . . . . nineteen
diciassette *(dee-chahs-set-teh)* . . . . seventeen
diciotto *(dee-choht-toh)* . . . . eighteen
dieci *(dee-eh-chee)* . . . . ten
dietro *(dee-eh-troh)* . . . . behind
difficile *(dee-fee-chee-leh)* . . . . difficult
dire *(dee-reh)* . . . . to say
  si dice *(see)(dee-cheh)* . . . . one says
diretto *(dee-ret-toh)* . . . . direct
direzione, la *(dee-reh-tsee-oh-neh)* . . . . direction
diritto *(dee-reet-toh)* . . . . straight ahead
disastro, il *(dee-zah-stroh)* . . . . accident, disaster
disco di sosta, il *(dee-skoh)(dee)(soh-stah)* . . . . . parking disk
distanza, la *(dee-stahn-tsah)* . . . . distance
divertimento, il *(dee-vair-tee-men-toh)* . . . . fun
divino *(dee-vee-noh)* . . . . divine
dizionario, il *(dee-tsee-oh-nah-ree-oh)* . . . . dictionary
doccia, la *(doh-chah)* . . . . shower
dodici *(doh-dee-chee)* . . . . twelve
dogana, la *(doh-gah-nah)* . . . . customs
dolce, il *(dohl-cheh)* . . . . sweet
dollaro, il *(dohl-lah-roh)* . . . . dollar
domanda, la *(doh-mahn-dah)* . . . . question
domani *(doh-mah-nee)* . . . . tomorrow
domenica *(doh-meh-nee-kah)* . . . . Sunday
dormire *(dor-mee-reh)* . . . . to sleep
dottore, il *(doht-toh-reh)* . . . . doctor
dove *(doh-veh)* . . . . where
  dov'è *(doh-veh)* . . . . where is
dovere *(doh-veh-reh)* . . . . to have to, must, to owe
dubbio, il *(doob-bee-oh)* . . . . doubt
due *(doo-eh)* . . . . two
durante *(doo-rahn-teh)* . . . . during
durare *(doo-rah-reh)* . . . . to last

E

e *(eh)* . . . . and
e mezzo *(eh)(med-zoh)* . . . . half past
e un quarto *(eh)(oon)(kwar-toh)* . . . . a quarter past
è *(eh)* . . . . (it) is
ebreo *(eh-breh-oh)* . . . . Jewish
eccellente *(eh-chel-len-teh)* . . . . excellent
ecco *(ek-koh)* . . . . here is, here are
economia, l' *(eh-koh-noh-mee-ah)* . . . . economy
economico *(eh-koh-noh-mee-koh)* . . . . inexpensive
edicola, l' *(eh-dee-koh-lah)* . . . . newsstand
Egitto, l' *(eh-jeet-toh)* . . . . Egypt
elenco telefonico, l' *(eh-len-koh)(teh-leh-foh-nee-koh)* . . . .
. . . . telephone book
email, l' *(ee-mail)* . . . . email
entrare *(en-trah-reh)* . . . . to enter
  entrata, l' *(en-trah-tah)* . . . . entrance
  entrata principale, l' *(en-trah-tah)(preen-chee-pah-leh)* . . . .
. . . . main entrance
era *(eh-rah)* . . . . was
esempio, l' *(eh-zem-pee-oh)* . . . . example

esperienza, la *(eh-speh-ree-en-tsah)* . . . . experience
est, l' *(est)* . . . . east
estate, l' *(eh-stah-teh)* . . . . summer
euro, l' *(eh-oo-roh)* . . . . euro
Europa, l' *(eh-oo-roh-pah)* . . . . Europe
europeo *(eh-oo-roh-peh-oh)* . . . . European

F

facchino, il *(fahk-kee-noh)* . . . . porter
fame, la *(fah-meh)* . . . . hunger
famiglia, la *(fah-meel-yah)* . . . . family
famoso *(fah-moh-zoh)* . . . . famous
farcito *(far-chee-toh)* . . . . stuffed
fare *(fah-reh)* . . . . to do, to make
  faccio *(fah-choh)* . . . . I make
fare la valigie *(fah-reh)(leh)(vah-lee-jeh)* . . . . to pack
farmacia, la *(far-mah-chee-ah)* . . . . pharmacy, drugstore
favore, il *(fah-voh-reh)* . . . . favor
fax, il *(fahx)* . . . . fax
fazzoletto, il *(fah-tsoh-let-toh)* . . . . handkerchief
febbraio *(feb-bry-oh)* . . . . February
fede, la *(feh-deh)* . . . . faith
fermata, la *(fair-mah-tah)* . . . . stop
Festa del Lavoro *(fes-tah)(del)(lah-voh-roh)* . . . . . . Labor Day
Festa della Resistenza *(fes-tah)(del-lah)(reh-zee-sten-tsah)* . . .
. . . . Liberation Day
figli, i *(feel-yee)* . . . . children
figlia, la *(feel-yah)* . . . . daughter
figlio, il *(feel-yoh)* . . . . son
film, il *(feelm)* . . . . film
filtro, il *(feel-troh)* . . . . filter
finalmente *(fee-nahl-men-teh)* . . . . finally
fine, la *(fee-neh)* . . . . end
finestra, la *(fee-neh-strah)* . . . . window
finito *(fee-nee-toh)* . . . . finished, ended
fioraio, il *(fee-oh-rye-yoh)* . . . . florist
fiore, il *(fee-oh-reh)* . . . . flower
fontana, la *(fohn-tah-nah)* . . . . fountain
forchetta, la *(for-ket-tah)* . . . . fork
foresta, la *(foh-reh-stah)* . . . . forest
forma, la *(for-mah)* . . . . form
formaggio, il *(for-mah-joh)* . . . . cheese
fra *(frah)* . . . . between
francese, il *(frahn-cheh-zeh)* . . . . French
Francia, la *(frahn-chah)* . . . . France
francobollo, il *(frahn-koh-bohl-loh)* . . . . stamp
fratello, il *(frah-tel-loh)* . . . . brother
freddo *(fred-doh)* . . . . cold
fresco *(freh-skoh)* . . . . cool, fresh
frigorifero, il *(free-goh-ree-feh-roh)* . . . . refrigerator
fritto *(freet-toh)* . . . . fried
frutta, la *(froot-tah)* . . . . fruit
fruttivendolo, il *(froot-tee-ven-doh-loh)* . . . . greengrocer
fumare *(foo-mah-reh)* . . . . to smoke
fuoco, il *(fwoh-koh)* . . . . fire, fire brigade

G

gabinetto, il *(gah-bee-net-toh)* . . . . lavatory, restroom
galleria, la *(gahl-leh-ree-ah)* . . . . gallery, tunnel
garage, il *(gah-rahzh)* . . . . garage
gatto, il *(gaht-toh)* . . . . cat
generalmente *(jeh-neh-rahl-men-teh)* . . . . generally
genitori, i *(jeh-nee-toh-ree)* . . . . parents
gennaio *(jen-ny-oh)* . . . . January
gentile *(jen-tee-leh)* . . . . kind, gentle
geografia, la *(jeh-oh-grah-fee-ah)* . . . . geography

geometria, la *(jeh-oh-meh-tree-ah)* . . . . geometry
Germania, la *(jair-mahn-yah)* . . . . Germany
giacca, la *(jahk-kah)* . . . . jacket
giallo *(jahl-loh)* . . . . yellow
Giappone, il *(jahp-poh-neh)* . . . . Japan
giaponese *(jahp-poh-neh-zeh)* . . . . Japanese
giardino, il *(jar-dee-noh)* . . . . garden
gioielli, i *(joy-el-lee)* . . . . jewelry
giornale, il *(jor-nah-leh)* . . . . newspaper
giorno, il, *(jor-noh)* . . . . day
giovane *(joh-vah-neh)* . . . . young
giovedì *(joh-veh-dee)* . . . . Thursday
giri *(jee-ree)* . . . . turn
giugno *(joon-yoh)* . . . . June
gli *(l-yee)* . . . . the
golfino, il *(gohl-fee-noh)* . . . . sweater
gondola, la *(gohn-doh-lah)* . . . . Venetian boat
gonna, la *(gohn-nah)* . . . . skirt
governo, il *(goh-vair-noh)* . . . . government
grado, il *(grah-doh)* . . . . degree
grande *(grahn-deh)* . . . . grand, big, large
grande magazzino, il *(grahn-deh)(mah-gah-tsee-noh)* . . . .
. . . . department store
grazie *(grah-tsee-eh)* . . . . thank you
Grecia, la *(greh-chah)* . . . . Greece
greco *(greh-koh)* . . . . Greek
grigio *(gree-joh)* . . . . gray
guanto, il *(gwahn-toh)* . . . . glove
guida, la *(gwee-dah)* . . . . guide

H

ha *(ah)* . . . . (he, she, it) has
ho *(oh)* . . . . I have
ho fame *(oh)(fah-meh)* . . . . I'm hungry
ho perso il mio *(oh)(pair-soh)(eel)(mee-oh)* . . I have lost my
ho sete *(oh)(seh-teh)* . . . . I'm thirsty

I – J

i *(ee)* . . . . the (plural)
idea, l' *(ee-deh-ah)* . . . . idea
ieri *(ee-eh-ree)* . . . . yesterday
il *(eel)* . . . . the (singular)
Immacolata Concezione *(eem-mah-koh-lah-tah)(kohn-cheh-tsee-oh-neh)* . . . . Immaculate Conception
imparare *(eem-pah-rah-reh)* . . . . to learn
impermeabile, l' *(eem-pair-meh-ah-bee-leh)* . . . . raincoat
importante *(eem-por-tahn-teh)* . . . . important
in *(een)* . . . . to, in, into
incantevole *(een-kahn-teh-vol-leh)* . . . . . enchanting, charming
incrocio, il *(een-kroh-choh)* . . . . crossing, junction
indirizzo, l' *(een-dee-ree-tsoh)* . . . . address
indispensabile *(een-dee-spen-sah-bee-leh)* . . . . . indispensable
individuo, l' *(een-dee-vee-doo-oh)* . . . . individual
industria, l' *(een-doo-stree-ah)* . . . . industry
industrioso *(een-doo-stree-oh-zoh)* . . . . industrious
influenza, l' *(een-floo-en-tsah)* . . . . influence
informazione, l' *(een-for-mah-tsee-oh-neh)* . . . . . . information
ingegnere, l' *(een-jen-yeh-reh)* . . . . engineer
Inghilterra, l' *(een-gheel-tair-rah)* . . . . England
inglese *(een-gleh-zeh)* . . . . English
ingresso, l' *(een-gres-soh)* . . . . entrance
innamorato *(een-nah-moh-rah-toh)* . . . . . . enamored, in love
insalata, l' *(een-sah-lah-tah)* . . . . salad
interamente *(een-teh-rah-men-teh)* . . . . entirely
interessante *(een-teh-res-sahn-teh)* . . . . interesting
internazionale *(een-tair-nah-tsee-oh-nah-leh)* . . . international

inverno, l' *(een-vair-noh)* . . . . winter
invito, l' *(een-vee-toh)* . . . . invitation
io *(ee-oh)* I
io sono *(ee-oh)(soh-noh)* . . . . I am
Irlanda, l' *(eer-lahn-dah)* . . . . Ireland
irlandsi, *(eer-lahnd-see)* . . . . Irish
Israele, l' *(eez-rah-eh-leh)* . . . . Israel
Italia, l' *(ee-tahl-yah)* . . . . Italy
Italiani, gli *(ee-tahl-yah-nee)* . . . . Italians
italiano *(ee-tahl-yah-noh)* . . . . Italian
jeans, i *(jeans)* . . . . jeans

L

l' *(l)* . . . . the (singular)
la *(lah)* . . . . the (singular)
lago, il *(lah-goh)* . . . . lake
lampada, la *(lahm-pah-dah)* . . . . lamp
largo *(lar-goh)* . . . . wide, broad
latte, il *(laht-teh)* . . . . milk
latteria, la *(laht-teh-ree-ah)* . . . . dairy
lavanderia, la *(lah-vahn-deh-ree-ah)* . . . . laundry
lavandino, il *(lah-vahn-dee-noh)* . . . . sink
lavare *(lah-vah-reh)* . . . . to wash
le *(leh)* . . . . the (plural)
leggere *(leh-jeh-reh)* . . . . to read
legume, il *(leh-goo-meh)* . . . . vegetable
lei *(leh-ee)* . . . . she
Lei *(leh-ee)* . . . . you (singular)
lentamente *(len-tah-men-teh)* . . . . slowly
lento *(len-toh)* . . . . slow
lettera, la *(let-teh-rah)* . . . . letter
letto, il *(let-toh)* . . . . bed
lezione, la *(leh-tsee-oh-neh)* . . . . lesson, lecture
lì *(lee)* . . . . there
libero *(lee-beh-roh)* . . . . free, liberated
libertà, la *(lee-bair-tah)* . . . . liberty
libreria, la *(lee-breh-ree-ah)* . . . . bookstore
libro, il *(lee-broh)* . . . . book
linea, la *(lee-neh-ah)* . . . . line
lingua, la *(leen-gwah)* . . . . language
lista, la *(lee-stah)* . . . . list, menu
litro, il *(lee-troh)* . . . . liter
lo *(loh)* . . . . it, the (singular)
locale *(loh-kah-leh)* . . . . local
loro *(loh-roh)* . . . . they, their
lotteria, la *(loht-teh-ree-ah)* . . . . lottery
luglio *(lool-yoh)* . . . . July
lui *(loo-ee)* . . . . he, him
lunedì *(loo-neh-dee)* . . . . Monday
lungo *(loon-goh)* . . . . long

M

macchina, la *(mahk-kee-nah)* . . . . car
macchina da noleggiare, la *(mahk-kee-nah)(dah)(noh-leh-jah-reh)* . . . . rental car
macchina fotografica, la *(mahk-kee-nah)(foh-toh-grah-fee-kah)* . . . . camera
macelleria, la *(mah-chel-leh-ree-ah)* . . . . butcher shop
madre, la *(mah-dreh)* . . . . mother
maestro, il *(mah-eh-stroh)* . . . . master, teacher
maggio *(mah-joh)* . . . . May
maglietta, la *(mahl-yet-tah)* . . . . T-shirt
magnifico *(mahn-yee-fee-koh)* . . . . magnificent
maiale, il *(my-ah-leh)* . . . . pork
malato *(mah-lah-toh)* . . . . sick

male (mah-leh) . . . . bad
mancia, la (mahn-chah) . . . . tip
mandare (mahn-dah-reh) . . . . to send
mangiare (mahn-jah-reh) . . . . to eat
maniera, la (mah-nee-eh-rah) . . . . manner, way
manzo, il (mahn-tsoh) . . . . beef
marciapiede, il (mar-chah-pee-eh-deh) . . . . . railway platform
mare, il (mah-reh) . . . . sea
marrone (mar-roh-neh) . . . . brown
marzo (mar-tsoh) . . . . March
martedì (mar-teh-dee) . . . . Tuesday
matita, la (mah-tee-tah) . . . . pencil
matrimonio, il (mah-tree-moh-nee-oh) . . . . marriage, wedding
mattina, la (maht-tee-nah) . . . . morning
medico, il (meh-dee-koh) . . . . physician
mela, la (meh-lah) . . . . apple
memoria, la (meh-moh-ree-ah) . . . . memory
meno (meh-noh) . . . . less, minus
   meno un quarto (meh-noh)(oon)(kwar-toh) . . . . a quarter to
menù, il (meh-noo) . . . . menu
meraviglioso (meh-rah-veel-yoh-zoh) . . . . marvelous
mercato, il (mair-kah-toh) . . . . market
mercoledì (mair-koh-leh-dee) . . . . Wednesday
mese, il, (meh-zeh) . . . . month
metallo, il (meh-tahl-loh) . . . . metal
metro, il (meh-troh) . . . . meter
metrò, il (meh-troh) . . . . subway
mezzanotte, la (med-zah-noht-teh) . . . . midnight
mezzo (med-zoh) . . . . middle
mezzogiorno, il (med-zoh-jor-noh) . . . . noon
mi chiamo (mee)(kee-ah-moh) . . . . my name is
mi dia (mee)(dee-ah) . . . . give me
mi dispiace (mee)(dee-spee-ah-cheh) . . . . I'm sorry
mi scriva (mee)(skree-vah) . . . . write for me
mi scusi (mee)(skoo-zee) . . . . excuse me
mi sono perso (mee)(soh-noh)(pair-soh) . . . . I'm lost
mila (mee-lah) . . . . thousand (two or more)
milione (meel-yoh-neh) . . . . million
mille (meel-leh) . . . . one thousand
minestra, la (mee-neh-strah) . . . . soup
minuto, il (mee-noo-toh) . . . . minute
mio (mee-oh) . . . . my
misura, la (mee-zoo-rah) . . . . measure, size
moda, la (moh-dah) . . . . style, fashion
molto (mohl-toh) . . . . very, a lot
momento, il (moh-men-toh) . . . . moment
moneta, la (moh-neh-tah) . . . . coin
montagna, la (mohn-tahn-yah) . . . . mountain
montone, il (mohn-toh-neh) . . . . mutton
moto, la (moh-toh) . . . . motorcycle
motocicletta, la (moh-toh-chee-klet-tah) . . . . motorcycle
motore, il (moh-toh-reh) . . . . motor, engine
multicolore (mool-tee-koh-loh-reh) . . . . multi-colored
museo, il (moo-zeh-oh) . . . . museum
musica, la (moo-zee-kah) . . . . music
mutande, le (moo-tahn-deh) . . . . underpants (♀)
mutandine, le (moo-tahn-dee-neh) . . . . underpants (♂)

<h1 style="text-align:center">N</h1>

Natale (nah-tah-leh) . . . . Christmas
nativo (nah-tee-voh) . . . . native
naturale (nah-too-rah-leh) . . . . natural
nave, la (nah-veh) . . . . ship
nazionale (nah-tsee-oh-nah-leh) . . . . national
nazione, la (nah-tsee-oh-neh) . . . . nation, country
necessario (neh-ches-sah-ree-oh) . . . . necessary

negozio, il (neh-goh-tsee-oh) . . . . store
nel, nella (nel)(nel-lah) . . . . in the
nero (neh-roh) . . . . black
nevica (neh-vee-kah) . . . . it snows
niente (nee-en-teh) . . . . nothing
no (noh) . . . . no
noi (noy) . . . . we
nome, il (noh-meh) . . . . name
non (nohn) . . . . not, no
   non me piace (nohn)(mee)(pee-ah-cheh) . . . . I do not like it
nonna, la (nohn-nah) . . . . grandmother
nonno, il (nohn-noh) . . . . grandfather
nord, il (nord) . . . . north
normale (nor-mah-leh) . . . . normal
notizia, la (noh-tee-tsee-ah) . . . . news, notice
notte, la (noht-teh) . . . . night
novanta (noh-vahn-tah) . . . . ninety
nove (noh-veh) . . . . nine
novembre (noh-vem-breh) . . . . November
numero, il (noo-meh-roh) . . . . number
nuovo (noo-oh-voh) . . . . new

<h1 style="text-align:center">O</h1>

o (oh) . . . . or
occasione, l' (ohk-kah-zee-oh-neh) . . . . . occasion, opportunity
occhiali, gli (ohk-kee-ah-lee) . . . . eyeglasses
occhiali da sole, gli (ohk-kee-ah-lee)(dah)(soh-leh) . . . sunglasses
occupato (ohk-koo-pah-toh) . . . . occupied
odore, l' (oh-doh-reh) . . . . odor (smell)
oggetto, l' (oh-jet-toh) . . . . object
oggi (oh-jee) . . . . today
ogni (ohn-yee) . . . . each, every
ogni quanto (ohn-yee)(kwahn-toh) . . . . how often
Ognissanti (ohn-yees-sahn-tee) . . . . All Saints' Day
ombrello, l' (ohm-brel-loh) . . . . umbrella
opera, l' (oh-peh-rah) . . . . opera
ora, la (oh-rah) . . . . hour
orario, l' (oh-rah-ree-oh) . . . . timetable
ordinare (or-dee-nah-reh) . . . . to order
ordinario (or-dee-nah-ree-oh) . . . . ordinary
orologeria, l' (oh-roh-loh-jeh-ree-ah) . . . .
   . . . . clock and watchmaker's shop
orologio, l' (oh-roh-loh-joh) . . . . clock
ospedale, l' (oh-speh-dah-leh) . . . . hospital
osteria, l' (oh-steh-ree-ah) . . . . cafe
ottanta (oht-tahn-tah) . . . . eighty
ottico, l' (oht-tee-koh) . . . . camera store
otto (oht-toh) . . . . eight
ottobre (oht-toh-breh) . . . . October
ovest, l' (oh-vest) . . . . west

<h1 style="text-align:center">P</h1>

pacco, il (pahk-koh) . . . . package
padre, il (pah-dreh) . . . . father
pagare (pah-gah-reh) . . . . to pay
pagina, la (pah-jee-nah) . . . . page
paio, il (pie-yoh) . . . . pair
palazzo, il (pah-lah-tsoh) . . . . palace
pane, il (pah-neh) . . . . bread
panetteria, la (pah-net-teh-ree-ah) . . . . bakery
pantofole, le (pahn-toh-foh-leh) . . . . slippers
pantaloni, i (pahn-tah-loh-nee) . . . . trousers
Papa, il (pah-pah) . . . . Pope
parcheggio, il (par-keh-joh) . . . . parking lot
parchimetro, il (par-kee-meh-troh) . . . . parking meter

parco, il (par-koh) . . . . park
parenti, i (pah-ren-tee) . . . . relatives
parlare (par-lah-reh) . . . . to speak
parola, la (pah-roh-lah) . . . . word
parole crociate, le (pah-roh-leh)(kroh-chah-teh) . . . .
. . . . crossword puzzle
parrucchiere, il (par-rook-kee-eh-reh) . . . . hairdresser
parte, la (par-teh) . . . . part, portion
partenza, la (par-ten-tsah) . . . . departure
partire (par-tee-reh) . . . . to leave, to depart
Pasqua (pah-skwah) . . . . Easter
passaporto, il (pahs-sah-por-toh) . . . . passport
pasta, la (pah-stah) . . . . pastry, pasta
pastasciutta, la (pah-stah-shoot-tah) . . . . pasta
pasticceria, la (pah-stee-cheh-ree-ah) . . . . pastry shop
pasto, il (pah-stoh) . . . . meal
patata, la (pah-tah-tah) . . . . potato
pelletteria, la (pel-let-tair-ee-ah) . . . . leather goods
penna, la (pen-nah) . . . . pen
pepe, il (peh-peh) . . . . pepper
per (pair) . . . . for
    per favore (pair)(fah-voh-reh) . . . . please
    per piacere (pair)(pee-ah-cheh-reh) . . . please, if you please
perché (pair-keh) . . . . why
perdere (pair-deh-reh) . . . . to lose
perfetto (pair-fet-toh) . . . . perfect
periodo, il (peh-ree-oh-doh) . . . . period
permanenza, la (pair-mah-nen-tsah) . . . . . stay, permanence
permesso, il (pair-mes-soh) . . . . permission
persona, la (pair-soh-nah) . . . . person
pesce, il (peh-sheh) . . . . fish
pescheria, la (peh-skeh-ree-ah) . . . . fish store
pettine, il (pet-tee-neh) . . . . comb
pezzo, il (peh-tsoh) . . . . piece
piacere, il (pee-ah-cheh-reh) . . . . pleasure
    Molto piacere (mohl-toh)(pee-ah-cheh-reh) . . . .
    . . . . It's a pleasure to meet you.
piano, il (pee-ahn-oh) . . . . floor
pianta, la (pee-ahn-tah) . . . . map
pianterreno, il (pee-ahn-tair-reh-noh) . . . . ground floor
piatto, il (pee-aht-toh) . . . . plate, dish
    piatto del giorno, il (pee-aht-toh)(del)(jor-noh) . . daily special
piazza, la (pee-ah-tsah) . . . . plaza, town square
piccolo (peek-koh-loh) . . . . little
pigiama, il (pee-jah-mah) . . . . pajamas
pillola, la (peel-loh-lah) . . . . pill
piove (pee-oh-veh) . . . . it rains
pittoresco (peet-toh-reh-skoh) . . . . picturesque
poco (poh-koh) . . . . a little
poco caro (poh-koh)(kah-roh) . . . . inexpensive
poi (poy) . . . . then
polizia, la (poh-lee-tsee-ah) . . . . police
pollame, il (pohl-lah-meh) . . . . poultry
pomeriggio, il (poh-meh-ree-joh) . . . . afternoon
ponte, il (pohn-teh) . . . . bridge
porta, la (por-tah) . . . . door
portafoglio, il (por-tah-fohl-yoh) . . . . wallet
porto, il (por-toh) . . . . port
Portogallo, il (por-toh-gahl-loh) . . . . Portugal
portoghese (por-toh-geh-zeh) . . . . Portuguese
porzione, la (por-tsee-oh-neh) . . . . portion
possibile (pohs-see-bee-leh) . . . . possible
posta, la (poh-stah) . . . . mail, post office
posteggio, il (poh-steh-joh) . . . . parking place
posto, il (poh-stoh) . . . . seat

potere (poh-teh-reh) . . . . to be able to, can
povero (poh-veh-roh) . . . . poor
pranzo, il (prahn-tsoh) . . . . lunch
precedente (preh-cheh-den-teh) . . . . preceding
preciso (preh-chee-zoh) . . . . precise, exact
prego (preh-goh) . . . . you're welcome
prendere (pren-deh-reh) . . . . to take
prenotare (preh-noh-tah-reh) . . . . to reserve, to book
prenotazione, la (preh-noh-tah-tsee-oh-neh) . . . . . reservation
preposizione, la (preh-poh-zee-tsee-oh-neh) . . . . . preposition
presente (preh-zen-teh) . . . . present
prezioso (preh-tsee-oh-zoh) . . . . precious, valuable
prezzo, il (preh-tsoh) . . . . price
prima colazione, la (pree-mah)(koh-lah-tsee-oh-neh) . . . breakfast
primavera, la (pree-mah-veh-rah) . . . . spring
problema, il (proh-bleh-mah) . . . . problem
profumi, i (proh-foo-mee) . . . . perfume
pronto (prohn-toh) . . . . prompt, ready
    Pronto! . . . . Hello! (when answering telephone)
protestante (proh-teh-stahn-teh) . . . . Protestant
puliti (poo-lee-tee) . . . . clean

Q

quadro, il (kwah-droh) . . . . picture
qual (kwahl) . . . . what, which
qualifica, la (kwah-lee-fee-kah) . . . . qualification
qualità, la (kwah-lee-tah) . . . . quality
quando (kwahn-doh) . . . . when
quante (kwahn-teh) . . . . how many
quanti (kwahn-tee) . . . . how many
quantità, la (kwahn-tee-tah) . . . . quantity
quanto (kwahn-toh) . . . . how much
    Quanto costa? (kwahn-toh)(koh-stah) . . . .
    . . . . How much does it cost?
quaranta (kwah-rahn-tah) . . . . forty
quartiere, il (kwar-tee-eh-reh) . . . . quarter, district
quarto, un (kwar-toh) . . . . quarter, fourth
    e un quarto (eh)(oon)(kwar-toh) . . . . . . a quarter past
quattordici (kwaht-tor-dee-chee) . . . . fourteen
quattro (kwaht-troh) . . . . four
quattrocento (kwaht-troh-chen-toh) . . . . four hundred
quello (kwel-loh) . . . . that
questo (kwes-toh) . . . . this
qui (kwee) . . . . here
quindici (kween-dee-chee) . . . . fifteen

R

radio, la (rah-dee-oh) . . . . radio
ragazza, la (rah-gah-tsah) . . . . girl
ragazzo, il (rah-gah-tsoh) . . . . boy
ragione, la (rah-joh-neh) . . . . reason
rapido (rah-pee-doh) . . . . rapid, fast
rasoio, il (rah-zoy-oh) . . . . razor
recente (reh-chen-teh) . . . . recent
reggipetto, il (reh-jee-pet-toh) . . . . brassière
religione, la (reh-lee-joh-neh) . . . . religion
resto, il (reh-stoh) . . . . rest, change (money)
ricco (reek-koh) . . . . rich
ricetta, la (ree-chet-tah) . . . . recipe
ricordo, il (ree-kor-doh) . . . . souvenir, record
Rinascimento, il (ree-nah-shee-men-toh) . . . . Renaissance
ripeta (ree-peh-tah) . . . . repeat
ripetere (ree-peh-teh-reh) . . . . to repeat
riso, il (ree-zoh) . . . . rice

rispetto, il *(ree-spet-toh)* . . . . respect
risposta, la *(ree-spoh-stah)* . . . . answer
ristorante, il *(ree-stoh-rahn-teh)* . . . . restaurant
ritardo *(ree-tar-doh)* . . . . late
rivista, la *(ree-vee-stah)* . . . . magazine
Roma *(roh-mah)* . . . . Rome
rosa *(roh-zah)* . . . . pink
rosa, la *(roh-zah)* . . . . rose
rosso *(rohs-soh)* . . . . red
rullino, il *(rool-lee-noh)* . . . . film
Russia, la *(roo-see-ah)* . . . . Russia
russo, il *(roos-soh)* . . . . Russian

S

sabato *(sah-bah-toh)* . . . . Saturday
sacco, il *(sahk-koh)* . . . . sack, bag
sala d'aspetto, la *(sah-lah)(dah-spet-toh)* . . . . . . waiting room
sala da pranzo, la *(sah-lah)(dah)(prahn-tsoh)* . . . . dining room
sale, il *(sah-leh)* . . . . salt
salotto, il *(sah-loht-toh)* . . . . living room
salsa, la *(sahl-sah)* . . . . sauce
salumeria, la *(sah-loo-meh-ree-ah)* . . . . delicatessen
salute, la *(sah-loo-teh)* . . . . health
    in buona salute *(een)(bwoh-nah)(sah-loo-teh)* . . . . . . healthy
saluto, il *(sah-loo-toh)* . . . . greeting, salutation
sandali, i *(sahn-dah-lee)* . . . . sandals
sapere *(sah-peh-reh)* . . . . to know (a fact)
sapone, il *(sah-poh-neh)* . . . . soap
scala, la *(skah-lah)* . . . . staircase, stairs
    La Scala *(skah-lah)* . . . . opera house in Milan
scarpe, le *(skar-peh)* . . . . shoes
scarpe da tennis, le *(skar-peh)(dah)(ten-nees)* . . . tennis shoes
scavo, lo *(skah-voh)* . . . . excavation
scena, la *(sheh-nah)* . . . . scene
scienza, la *(shee-en-zah)* . . . . science
scrivania, la *(skree-vah-nee-ah)* . . . . desk
scrivere *(skree-veh-reh)* . . . . to write
scuola, la *(skoo-oh-lah)* . . . . school
secondo *(seh-kohn-doh)* . . . . second (as in first and second)
secondo, il *(seh-kohn-doh)* . . . . second (time)
sedia, la *(seh-dee-ah)* . . . . chair
sedici *(seh-dee-chee)* . . . . sixteen
seduto *(seh-doo-tah)* . . . . seated
segnale, il *(sen-yah-leh)* . . . . signal, sign
segretario, il *(seh-greh-tah-ree-oh)* . . . . secretary (male)
seguente *(seh-gwen-teh)* . . . . following
sei *(seh-ee)* . . . . six
selezione, la *(seh-leh-tsee-oh-neh)* . . . . selection, choice
semisfera, la *(seh-mee-sfeh-rah)* . . . . hemisphere
sempre *(sem-preh)* . . . . always
sentimento, il *(sen-tee-men-toh)* . . . . feeling
senza *(sen-zah)* . . . . without
sera, la *(seh-rah)* . . . . evening
serio *(seh-ree-oh)* . . . . serious
servizio, il *(sair-vee-tsee-oh)* . . . . service
sessanta *(ses-sahn-tah)* . . . . sixty
settanta *(set-tahn-tah)* . . . . seventy
sette *(set-teh)* . . . . seven
settembre *(set-tem-breh)* . . . . September
settimana, la *(set-tee-mah-nah)* . . . . week
sfortunato *(sfor-too-nah-toh)* . . . . unfortunate, unlucky
short, gli *(short)* . . . . shorts
sì *(see)* . . . . yes
Sicilia *(see-chee-lee-ah)* . . . . Sicily
sicuro *(see-koo-roh)* . . . . safe, sure, secure
sidro, il *(see-droh)* . . . . cider
114 sigaretta, la *(see-gah-ret-tah)* . . . . cigarette

sigaro, il *(see-gah-roh)* . . . . cigar
signor, il *(seen-yor)* . . . . Mr.
signora, la *(seen-yoh-rah)* . . . . lady, woman, Mrs.
signore, il *(seen-yoh-reh)* . . . . man
signorina, la *(seen-yoh-ree-nah)* . . . . Miss
simile *(see-mee-leh)* . . . . similar
similitudine, la *(see-mee-lee-too-dee-neh)* . . . . similarity
sincero *(seen-cheh-roh)* . . . . sincere
sinfonia, la *(seen-foh-nee-ah)* . . . . symphony
sinistra *(see-nee-strah)* . . . . left
sistema, il *(see-steh-mah)* . . . . system
sofà, il *(soh-fah)* . . . . sofa
soggetto, il *(soh-jet-toh)* . . . . subject
sole, il *(soh-leh)* . . . . sun
solo *(soh-loh)* . . . . alone, solitary
solo andata *(soh-loh)(ahn-dah-tah)* . . . . one-way (ticket)
sopra *(soh-prah)* . . . . over, above
    di sopra *(dee)(soh-prah)* . . . . above, upstairs
sorella, la *(soh-rel-lah)* . . . . sister
sorpresa, la *(sor-preh-zah)* . . . . surprise
sotto *(soht-toh)* . . . . under, below
    di sotto *(dee)(soht-toh)* . . . . below, downstairs
sottoveste, la *(soht-toh-veh-steh)* . . . . slip
Spagna, la *(spahn-yah)* . . . . Spain
spagnolo, lo *(spahn-yoh-loh)* . . . . Spanish, Spaniard
spazzolino da denti, lo *(spah-tsoh-lee-noh)(dah)(den-tee)* . . . .
. . . . toothbrush
specchio, lo *(spek-kee-oh)* . . . . mirror
spesso *(spes-soh)* . . . . often
spettacolo, lo *(spet-tah-koh-loh)* . . . . spectacle, show
spingere *(speen-jeh-reh)* . . . . to push (doors)
sportello, lo *(spor-tel-loh)* . . . . ticket window, counter
stagioni, le *(stah-joh-nee)* . . . . seasons
stanco *(stahn-koh)* . . . . tired
stanza, la *(stahn-zah)* . . . . room
Stati Uniti, gli *(stah-tee)(oo-nee-tee)* . . . . United States
stazione, la *(stah-tsee-oh-neh)* . . . . train station
stivali, gli *(stee-vah-lee)* . . . . boots
strada, la *(strah-dah)* . . . . street
straniero, lo *(strah-nee-eh-roh)* . . . . stranger, foreigner
straordinario *(strah-or-dee-nah-ree-oh)* . . . . . . extraordinary
studio, lo *(stoo-dee-oh)* . . . . study, studio
su *(soo)* . . . . on
successo, il *(soo-ches-soh)* . . . . success
succo, il *(soo-koh)* . . . . juice
sud, il *(sood)* . . . . south
sudafricano *(sood-ah-free-kah-noh)* . . . . South African
sul *(sool)* . . . . on the
sulla *(sool-lah)* . . . . on the
Suo *(soo-oh)* . . . . your
superiore *(soo-peh-ree-oh-reh)* . . . . superior, above
supermercato, il *(soo-pair-mair-kah-toh)* . . . . . . supermarket
sveglia, la *(zvel-yah)* . . . . alarm clock
Svizzera, la *(zveet-tsair-ah)* . . . . Switzerland
svizzero *(zveet-tsair-oh)* . . . . Swiss

T

tabaccheria, la *(tah-bahk-keh-ree-ah)* . . . . tobacco shop
tabacco, il *(tah-bahk-koh)* . . . . tobacco
taglia, la *(tahl-yah)* . . . . size
tappeto, il *(tahp-peh-toh)* . . . . carpet
tariffa, la *(tah-reef-fah)* . . . . fare
tassa, la *(tahs-sah)* . . . . tax
tassì, il *(tahs-see)* . . . . taxi
tavola calda, la *(tah-voh-lah)(kahl-dah)* . . . . cafeteria
tavolo, il *(tah-voh-loh)* . . . . table

tazza, la *(tah-tsah)* .... cup
tè, il *(teh)* .... tea
teatro, il *(teh-ah-troh)* .... theater
tedesco, il *(teh-deh-skoh)* .... German
telefono, il *(teh-leh-foh-noh)* .... telephone
telefonata, la *(teh-leh-foh-nah-tah)* .... telephone call
telefonino, il *(teh-leh-foh-nee-noh)* .... cellular telephone
televisione, la *(teh-leh-vee-zee-oh-neh)* .... television
temperatura, la *(tem-peh-rah-too-rah)* .... temperature
tempo, il *(tem-poh)* .... weather, time
tendina, la *(ten-dee-nah)* .... curtain
termometro, il *(tair-moh-meh-troh))* .... thermometer
terrazza, la *(tair-rah-tsah)* .... terrace
tesoro, il *(teh-zoh-roh)* .... treasure
tintoria, la *(teen-toh-ree-ah)* .... dry cleaner's
tipiche *(tee-pee-keh)* .... typical
tirare *(tee-rah-reh)* .... to pull (doors)
titolo, il *(tee-toh-loh)* .... title
torre, la *(tor-reh)* .... tower
   La Torre Pendente *(tor-reh)(pen-den-teh)* ....
.... Leaning Tower of Pisa
tovagliolo, il *(toh-vahl-yoh-loh)* .... napkin
tra *(trah)* .... between
tram, il *(trahm)* .... tram, street car
tranquillo *(trahn-kweel-loh)* .... calm, tranquil
trattoria, la *(traht-toh-ree-ah)* .... restaurant
travel check, i *(trah-vel)(check)* ...... traveler's checks
tre *(treh)* .... three
tredici *(treh-dee-chee)* .... thirteen
treno, il *(treh-noh)* .... train
trenta *(tren-tah)* .... thirty
trovare *(troh-vah-reh)* .... to find
tu *(too)* .... you (informal / singular)
Tunisia, la *(too-nee-zee-ah)* .... Tunisia
Turchia, la *(toor-kee-ah)* .... Turkey
turco *(toor-koh)* .... Turkish
turista, il *(too-ree-stah)* .... tourist
tutto *(toot-toh)* .... everything

U

ufficio, l' *(oof-fee-choh)* .... office
ufficio oggetti smarriti, l' *(oof-fee-choh)(oh-jet-tee)(zmar-ree-tee)* .... lost-and-found office
ufficio di cambio, l' *(oof-fee-choh)(dee)(kahm-bee-oh)* ....
.... money-exchange office
ufficio postale, l' *(oof-fee-choh)(poh-stah-leh)* ...... post office
ultimo *(ool-tee-moh)* .... last, ultimate, final
un, un' *(oon)* .... a
un po' *(oon)(poh)* .... a little
una *(oo-nah)* .... a
unico *(oo-nee-koh)* .... unique, only, single
  senso unico *(sen-soh)(oo-nee-koh)* .... one-way (traffic)
undici *(oon-dee-chee)* .... eleven
Ungheria, la *(oon-gair-ee-ah)* .... Hungary
universale *(oo-nee-vair-sah-leh)* .... universal
università, l' *(oo-nee-vair-see-tah)* .... university
uno *(oo-noh)* .... one, a
uova, le *(oo-oh-vah)* .... eggs
urbano *(oor-bah-noh)* .... urban
usato *(oo-zah-toh)* .... used, second-hand
uscire *(oo-shee-reh)* .... to go out, to exit
uscita, l' *(oo-shee-tah)* .... exit
uscita di sicurezza, l' *(oo-shee-tah)(dee)(see-koo-reh-tsah)* ....
.... emergency exit
usi *(oo-zee)* .... use
usuale *(oo-zoo-ah-leh)* .... usual, customary
utensile, l' *(oo-ten-see-leh)* .... utensil

V

vacanze, le *(vah-kahn-tseh)* .... vacation
vaccinazione, la *(vah-chee-nah-tsee-oh-neh)* ...... vaccination
vagone letto, il *(vah-goh-neh)(let-toh)* .... sleeping car
vagone ristorante, il *(vah-goh-neh)(ree-stoh-rahn-teh)* .....
.... dining car
valigia, la *(vah-lee-jah)* .... suitcase
vaniglia, la *(vah-neel-yah)* .... vanilla
vaporetto, il *(vah-poh-ret-toh)* .... steam ferry (in Venice)
varietà, la *(vah-ree-eh-tah)* .... variety
vaso, il *(vah-zoh)* .... vase
vecchio *(vek-kee-oh)* .... old
vedere *(veh-deh-reh)* .... to see
veloce *(veh-loh-cheh)* .... fast
vena, la *(veh-nah)* .... vein
vendere *(ven-deh-reh)* .... to sell
venditore, il *(ven-dee-toh-reh)* ..... vendor, seller
venerdì *(veh-nair-dee)* .... Friday
vengo *(ven-goh)* .... I come
venire *(veh-nee-reh)* .... to come
venti *(ven-tee)* .... twenty
vento, il *(ven-toh)* .... windy
verbo, il *(vair-boh)* .... verb
verde *(vair-deh)* .... green
verdura, la *(vair-doo-rah)* .... vegetable
vergine, la *(vair-jee-neh)* .... virgin
vero *(veh-roh)* .... true, real
versione, la *(vair-zee-oh-neh)* .... version
vestiti, i *(veh-stee-tee)* .... clothing
vestito, il *(veh-stee-toh)* .... dress
via *(vee-ah)* .... by
  via aerea *(vee-ah)(ah-eh-reh-ah)* .... by airmail
via, la *(vee-ah)* .... way
viaggiare *(vee-ah-jah-reh)* .... to travel
viaggiatore, il *(vee-ah-jah-toh-reh)* .... traveler
viaggio, il *(vee-ah-joh)* .... trip
viene *(vee-eh-neh)* .... come, comes
vietato *(vee-eh-tah-toh)* .... prohibited
  vietato entrare *(vee-eh-tah-toh)(en-trah-reh)* ... do not enter
vigoroso *(vee-goh-roh-zoh)* .... vigorous
vino, il *(vee-noh)* .... wine
violetto *(vee-oh-let-toh)* .... violet
visita, la *(vee-zee-tah)* .... visit
  fare una vista *(fah-reh)(oo-nah)(vee-zee-tah)* ... to pay a visit
visitare *(vee-zee-tah-reh)* .... to visit
vita, la *(vee-tah)* .... life
vitamina, la *(vee-tah-mee-nah)* ....vitamin
vitello, il *(vee-tel-loh)* .... veal
voi *(voy)* .... you (plural)
volere *(voh-leh-reh)* ....to want
voglio *(vohl-yoh)* .... want
volo, il *(voh-loh)* .... flight
vorrei *(vor-reh-ee)* .... I would like
vorremmo *(vor-rem-moh)* .... we would like

W – Z

W.C., il *(vee-chee)* .... toilet, water closet
zero *(zeh-roh)* .... zero
zia, la *(dzee-ah)* .... aunt
zio, lo *(dzee-oh)* .... uncle
zodiaco, lo *(zoh-dee-ah-koh)* .... zodiac
zona, la *(zoh-nah)* .... zone
zoo, lo *(dzoh)* .... zoo
zuppa, la *(zoop-pah)* .... soup

This beverage guide is intended to explain the variety of beverages available to you while **in Italia.** It is by no means complete. Some of the experimenting has been left up to you, but this should get you started.

BEVANDE CALDE (hot drinks)

caffè	coffee (espresso)
caffellatte	coffee with steamed milk
cappuccino	coffee with steamed milk and milk froth
caffè americano	American-style coffee
caffè macchiato	coffee with a little milk or cream
cioccolata	cocoa

tè	tea
tè con limone	tea with lemon
tè con latte	tea with milk

BEVANDE FREDDE (cold drinks)

latte freddo	cold milk
frappé	milkshake
succo	juice
succo di arancia	orange juice
acqua	water
acqua minerale	mineral water
amarena	cherry syrup drink
orzata	almond syrup drink
tè freddo	iced tea
caffè freddo	iced coffee
ghiaccio	ice

VINO (wine)

There is a wide variety of wines in Italy. Each region produces its own wine, ranging in taste from very sweet to very dry. You may drink wine by the **bicchiere** (glass), **litro** (liter), **mezzo litro** (half liter), or the **bottiglia** (bottle).

vino rosso	red wine
vino bianco	white wine
vino rosè	rosé wine
spumante	sparkling wine
vino ordinario	table wine
vino da tavola	table wine
vino della casa	house wine
vino locale	local wine of the region
dolce	sweet
amabile	between sweet and dry
secco	dry

BIRRA (beer)

There are many brands of beer. **Birra** is generally purchased **in bottiglia** (bottled) or **alla spina** (draught).

BEVANDE ALCOOLICHE (alcoholic beverages)

vodka	vodka
whisky	scotch
bourbon	bourbon
gin	gin
rum	rum
martini dry	American martini
acquavite	natural grain spirits
grappa	wine brandy
cognac	cognac

Il Menù

Preparazione (preparation)

cotto cooked
crudo raw
arrosto roasted
fritto fried
al forno baked
alla griglia, ai ferri grilled
allo spiedo roasted on a spit
bollito boiled
affumicato smoked
alla brace charcoal-broiled
farcito stuffed
al sangue rare
al punto medium
ben cotto well-done

Altri (others)

marmellata jam
miele honey
sale salt
pepe pepper
olio oil
aceto vinegar
senape/mostarda mustard
riso rice
pane bread
formaggio cheese
dolci desserts
torta cake
dolce pastry
gelato ice cream
panna montata whipped cream

FOLD HERE

Riso, Risotto (rice)

alla milanese with saffron
con funghi with mushrooms
alla marinara tomato sauce, clams, prawns

Frutta (fruit)

mela apple
pera pear
pesca peach
banana banana
arancia orange
mandarino tangerine
ciliegie cherries
cocomero watermelon
prugna plum
uva grapes
uva passa raisins
dattero date
limone lemon
ananas pineapple
pompelmo grapefruit
fichi figs
fragole strawberries
lamponi raspberries
mirtilli blueberries

Bevande (beverages)

birra beer
latte milk
caffè coffee
caffellatte coffee with steamed milk
succo di . . . juice of . . .
limonata lemonade
acqua minerale bottled mineral water
vino rosso red wine
vino bianco white wine
vino rosè rosé wine
light diet drinks

(bwohn) **Buon appetito!** *(ahp-peh-tee-toh)*
enjoy your meal

FOLD HERE

Pastasciutta (pasta)

spaghetti long, solid-core pasta
fettucine flat noodle
ravioli small, stuffed pasta square
lasagne baked, layered casserole
cannelloni stuffed cylinder-shaped pasta
tortellini small stuffed pasta
vermicelli very thin pasta
cannolo short tubes of macaroni
cappelletti round, cap-shaped pasta
conchiglie shell-shaped pasta
gnocchi small dumplings
linguine narrow, flat noodles
penne hollow pasta, cut diagonally
rigatoni large, hollow pasta

Verdura (vegetables)

cipolle onions
piselli green peas
pomodori tomatoes
fagiolini string beans
cavolfiore cauliflower
carciofo artichokes
carote carrots
asparagi asparagus
spinaci spinach
lenticchie lentils
funghi mushrooms
broccoli broccoli
melanzane eggplant
olive olives
patate potatoes
peperoni bell peppers
prezzemolo parsley
rapanelli radishes
sedano celery
zucca yellow squash
zucchini zucchini

Minestre e Zuppe (soups)

minestrone thick vegetable soup
minestrina thin clear broth
zuppa di pesce fish soup
stracciatella broth with beaten eggs and Parmesan cheese
pavese broth with poached egg on fried bread

Antipasti (appetizers)

acciughe	anchovies
di mare	seafood with lemon-juice dressing
misto	mixed appetizers
frutti di mare	seafood
gamberi	shrimps and prawns
lumache	snails
ostriche	oysters
peperonata	sliced peppers, onions and tomatoes
mortadella	bologna
prosciutto	ham
salame	variety of sausages
salsicce	cooked sausage

Insalate (salads)

verde	tossed green salad
capricciosa	mixed vegetables, with ham in mayonnaise sauce
di pesce	boiled fish
di riso	cold rice, vegetables, seafood, mayonnaise
mista	mixed green salad with tomatoes
viennese	tuna, hard-boiled eggs, beans, olives

Carne (meat)
Vitello (veal)

bistecca di vitello	loin veal steak
costoletta di vitello	veal chop or steak
coteletta	veal steak without bone
alla Milanese	breaded veal cutlets
lombata di vitello	loin of veal
noce di vitello	sirloin of veal
rollatine di vitello	rolled stuffed breast of veal
spalla di vitello al forno	roast shoulder of veal

Maiale (pork)

arrosto di maiale	roast loin of pork
arrostino alla salvia	roast pork with sage
arrosto di porchetta	stuffed roast suckling pig
zampe di maiale	pig's feet

Manzo (beef)

braciole	rib steak
entrecote	boneless rib steak
fegato	liver
cervella	brains
lingua di bue	beef tongue
stracotto	stew

Agnello (lamb)

abbacchio	milk-fed lamb
braciolette d'abbacchio	grilled lamb chops or cutlets
abbacchio al forno	roasted lamb
costole alla Milanese	fried breaded lamb chops
tracciole d'agnello	a type of shish kebab

Pollame (poultry)

pollo	chicken
tacchino	turkey
faraona	guinea fowl
cappone	capon
piccione	pigeon
quaglie	quail
fagiano	pheasant

Cacciagione (wild game)

anatra	duck
cervo	deer
coniglio	rabbit
lepre	hare
tordo	thrush

Pesci e Frutti di Mare (fish and seafood)

acciughe	anchovies
aragosta	lobster
calamari	squid
gamberi	shrimp or prawns
granchio	crab
merluzzo	codfish
cozze	mussels
persico	perch
pesce spada	swordfish
polipo	octopus
salmone	salmon
sardine	sardines
sogliola	sole
spigola	sea bass
storione	sturgeon
tonno	tuna
trota	trout
vongole	clams

Sugo di Carne (meat sauces)

alla Bolognese	meat and tomato sauce
alla Romagnola	tomato sauce with garlic and parsley
alla carbonara	sauce of eggs, bacon and garlic
alla Fiorentina	herbal meat sauce with green peas
all'arrabbiata	herbal tomato sauce of bacon, sausage and cayenne
alla Piemontese	herbal meat sauce with nutmeg and truffles
alla Romana	seasoned meat sauce

Senza Carne (meatless sauces)

aglio e olio	olive oil and garlic
alla besciamella	creamed white sauce
al burro	butter and Parmesan
alla Campagnola	mushrooms, tomatoes and herbs
alla crema	white sauce with egg yolk and Parmesan cheese
al pesto	basil, garlic and pine nuts
alla Napoletana	tomatoes, basil and Parmesan cheese
al pomodoro	herbal tomato sauce

Frutti di Mare (seafood sauces)

alla boscaiola	tuna, anchovies, tomatoes and mushrooms
ai frutti di mare	herbs, tomatoes and seafood
al tonno	tuna, garlic, tomatoes and capers
di magro	tuna, anchovies and herbs
alla posillipo	herbs, tomatoes and seafood
alle vongole	clams and garlic, with or without tomatoes

FOLD HERE

(ee-oh)
io

(noy)
noi

(loo-ee)
lui

(leh-ee)
Lei

(leh-ee)
lei

(loh-roh)
loro

(par-lah-reh)
parlare
(par-loh)
io parlo

(pren-deh-reh)
prendere
(pren-doh)
io prendo

(eem-pah-rah-reh)
imparare
(eem-pah-roh)
io imparo

(ah-bee-tah-reh)
abitare
(ah-bee-toh)
io abito

(kohm-prah-reh)
comprare
(kohm-proh)
io compro

(kee-ah-mar-see)
chiamarsi
(mee) *(kee-ah-moh)*
io mi chiamo

we	I
you	he
they	she
to take	to speak
I take	I speak
to live / reside	to learn
I live / reside	I learn
to be called	to buy
my name is . . .	I buy

(veh-nee-reh)
venire

(ven-goh)
io vengo

(ahn-dah-reh)
andare

(vah-doh)
io vado

(ah-veh-reh)
avere

(oh)
io ho

(ah-veh-reh) *(bee-zohn-yoh)* *(dee)*
avere bisogno di

(oh) *(bee-zohn-yoh)* *(dee)*
io ho bisogno di

(dee-reh)
dire

(dee-koh)
io dico

(vor-reh-ee)
vorrei

(mahn-jah-reh)
mangiare

(mahn-joh)
io mangio

(beh-reh)
bere

(beh-voh)
io bevo

(troh-vah-reh)
trovare

(troh-voh)
io trovo

(kah-pee-reh)
capire

(kah-pee-skoh)
io capisco

(ven-deh-reh)
vendere

(ven-doh)
io vendo

(ree-peh-teh-reh)
ripetere

(ree-peh-toh)
io ripeto

to go	to come
I go	I come
to have need of / need	to have
I need	I have
I would like	to say
	I say
to drink	to eat
I drink	I eat
to understand	to find
I understand	I find
to repeat	to sell
I repeat	I sell

(veh-deh-reh)
vedere

(veh-doh)
io vedo

(fah-reh)
fare

(fah-choh)
io faccio

(mahn-dah-reh)
mandare

(mahn-doh)
io mando

(dor-mee-reh)
dormire

(dor-moh)
io dormo

(ah-spet-tah-reh)
aspettare

(ah-spet-toh)
io aspetto

(leh-jeh-reh)
leggere

(leh-goh)
io leggo

(mee)   *(dee-ah)*
mi dia . . .

(skree-veh-reh)
scrivere

(skree-voh)
io scrivo

(pah-gah-reh)
pagare

(pah-goh)
io pago

(poh-teh-reh)
potere

(pohs-soh)
io posso

(doh-veh-reh)
dovere

(deh-voh)
io devo

(sah-peh-reh)
sapere

(soh)
io so

to do / make	to see
I do / make	I see
to sleep	to send
I sleep	I send
to read	to wait (for)
I read	I wait (for)
to write	give me . . .
I write	
to be able to / can	to pay (for)
I can	I pay (for)
to know (fact)	to have to/must/to owe
I know	I have to/must/owe

(preh-noh-tah-reh)
prenotare
(preh-noh-toh)
io prenoto

(ahn-dah-reh)   *(ah-eh-reh-oh)*
andare in aereo
(vah-doh)   *(ah-eh-reh-oh)*
io vado in aereo

(vee-ah-jah-reh)
viaggiare
(vee-ah-joh)
io viaggio

(par-tee-reh)
partire
(par-toh)
io parto

(ar-ree-vah-reh)
arrivare
(ar-ree-voh)
io arrivo

(kahm-bee-ah-reh)
cambiare
(kahm-bee-oh)
io cambio

(fah-reh) *(leh)* *(vah-lee-jeh)*
fare le valige
(fah-choh)   *(vah-lee-jeh)*
io faccio le valige

(doo-rah-reh)
durare
(doo-rah)
dura

(cheh)   *(chee)* *(soh-noh)*
c'è / ci sono

(leh-ee)   *(ah)*
Lei ha . . . ?

(lah-vah-reh)
lavare
(lah-voh)
io lavo

(or-dee-nah-reh)
ordinare
(or-dee-noh)
io ordino

to fly	to reserve / book
I fly	I reserve / book
to leave	to travel
I leave	I travel
to transfer (vehicles) / to change money	to arrive
I transfer / change money	I arrive
to last	to pack
(it) lasts	I pack
Do you have . . . ?	there is / there are
to order	to wash
I order	I wash

(oh-jee)
oggi

(koh-meh)   *(stah)*
Come sta?

(ee-eh-ree)
ieri

(pair)   *(fah-voh-reh)*
per favore

(doh-mah-nee)
domani

(grah-tsee-eh)
grazie

(chow)
ciao

(mee)   *(skoo-zee)*
mi scusi

(vek-kee-oh)   *(noo-oh-voh)*
vecchio - nuovo

(kwahn-toh)   *(koh-stah)*
Quanto costa?

(grahn-deh)   *(peek-koh-loh)*
grande - piccolo

(ah-pair-toh)   *(kee-oo-zoh)*
aperto - chiuso

How are you?	today
please	yesterday
thank you	tomorrow
excuse me	hi / bye
How much does this cost?	old - new
open - closed	large - small

(mah-lah-toh)   *(bwoh-nah)*   *(sah-loo-teh)*

malato - in buona salute

(bwoh-noh)   *(kaht-tee-voh)*

buono - cattivo

(kahl-doh)   *(fred-doh)*

caldo - freddo

(kor-toh)   *(loon-goh)*

corto - lungo

(ahl-toh)   *(bahs-soh)*

alto - basso

(soh-prah)   *(soht-toh)*

sopra - sotto

(see-nee-strah)   *(deh-strah)*

sinistra - destra

(veh-loh-cheh)   *(rah-pee-doh)*   *(len-toh)*

veloce / rapido - lento

(vek-kee-oh)   *(joh-vah-neh)*

vecchio - giovane

(eh-koh-noh-mee-koh)   *(kah-roh)*

economico - caro

(poh-veh-roh)   *(reek-koh)*

povero - ricco

(mohl-toh)   *(poh-koh)*

molto - poco

good - bad

ill - healthy

short - long

hot - cold

above - below

tall - short

fast - slow

left - right

inexpensive-
expensive

old - young

a lot - a little

poor - rich

Now that you've finished...

You've done it!

You've completed all the Steps, stuck your labels, flashed your cards, cut out your beverage and menu guides and practiced your new language. Do you realize how far you've come and how much you've learned? You've accomplished what it could take years to achieve in a traditional language class.

You can now confidently

- ask questions,
- understand directions,
- make reservations,
- order food and
- shop for anything.

And you can do it all in a foreign language! Go anywhere with confidence — from a large cosmopolitan restaurant to a small, out-of-the-way village where no one speaks English. Your experiences will be much more enjoyable and worry-free now that you speak the language.

As you've seen, learning a foreign language can be fun. Why limit yourself to just one? Now you're ready to learn another language with the *10 minutes a day*® Series!

Kris Kershul

Kristine Kershul

To place an order –

- Visit us at www.bbks.com, day or night.
- Call us at (800) 488-5068 or (206) 284-4211 between 8:00 a.m. and 5:00 p.m. Pacific Time, Monday - Friday.
- If you have questions about ordering, please call us. You may also fax us at (206) 284-3660 or email us at customer.service@bbks.com.

RUSSIAN
a language map

Contents

- Meeting People
- Asking Questions
- Numbers
- Telephone & Internet
- Mail
- Calendar & Time
- Shopping
- Alphabet
- Sightseeing
- Money
- Transportation
- Hotels
- Emergencies
- Dining Out

Tip: Pronounce the phonetics just as you see them. Don't over-analyze them. Speak with a Russian accent and, above all, enjoy yourself.

If you turn to the back of this *Language Map* you will find the native Russian alphabet in Russian alphabetical order for quick reference.

Language Map® Series

These handy *Language Maps*® provide over 1,000 words and phrases to cover the basics for any trip.

- Don't leave home without one! It's an absolute must-have for anyone traveling abroad.

- Snap-open-and-fold design allows for quick reference.

- Take it everywhere! Laminated to resist damage even under the toughest travel conditions.

Coming soon!

The *Grab and Go*™ Series is a traveler's dream come true!

ITALIAN
– grab and go™

- Audio CD
- ITALIAN *a language map*®
- Exclusive *Grab & Go*™ QuickCard Packets

Grab and Go™ Series

- Perfect for on-the-go travelers.

- A winning combination – a *Language Map*®, an audio CD and exclusive *Grab and Go*™ QuickCard Packets.

- Download it onto your MP3 player and you've got the essentials with you for any occasion.

10 minutes a day® AUDIO CD Series

The *10 minutes a day*® AUDIO CD Series is based on the ever-popular *10 minutes a day*® Series. Millions of people have used this program with great success!

- Demand the best! Excellent for the classroom, homeschoolers, business professionals and travelers.

- An entertaining program with eight hours of personal instruction on six CDs.

- Practice along with native speakers.

- Use the CDs with the companion book and maximize your progress!

GERMAN
in 10 minutes a day® AUDIO CD

COMPLETE WITH
- 6 Audio CDs • 132-page book which includes •
Sticky Labels • Flash Cards • Puzzles and Quizzes •
Menu Guide • Beverage Guide • Currency Guide •
Street Signs • Metric Tables • German-English Glossary